INSIGHT COMPACT GUIDES

Compact Guide: Rhodes is the ultimate quick-reference guide to this pearl of the Aegean. It tells you all you need to know about the island's many attractions, from its beautiful beaches to its crusader castles, from its pious pictures to its mythical mountains.

This is just one title in *Apa Publications'* new series of pocket-sized, easy-to-use guidebooks intended for the independent-minded traveller. Based on an award-winning formula pioneered in Germany, *Compact Guides* pride themselves on being up-to-date and authoritative. They are in essence mini travel encyclopedias, designed to be comprehensive yet portable, both readable and reliable.

Star Attractions

An instant reference to some of Rhodes' most popular tourist attractions to help you on your way.

Rhodes Old Town p17

Archaeological Museum p22

Turkish Quarter p27

Temple of Apollo p37

Kalithea Beach p39

Cape Ladiko p39

Thari Monastery p41

Kimisis Theotokou p41

Lindos p45

Valley of the Butterflies p49

Symi p62

RHODES

Introduction

Places

Culture

Leisure

Practical Information

Rhodes – the Island Blessed by Helios

Opposite: a local observer

In ancient times, the importance of Rhodes as a naval power and a prosperous trading post was attributable to the island's favourable strategic position close to Asia Minor and Egypt.

Centuries later, the thought of occupying such a position encouraged invading armies, and the Persians, Romans, Arabs, Knights of St John and the Ottoman Turks have all dominated the island at some time.

But Rhodes has always enjoyed the blessing of Helios, the sun god, and he too has played his part in creating such a prize. No other island in the Aegean enjoys 270 sunny days a year, as Rhodes does. Many people wonder why Rhodes, which means 'Rose Island' is so called when no roses grow there. The name probably derives from the wealth of natural, floral beauty to be found here. In spring, brightly coloured blossom in every imaginable shade of red adorns the island.

Spring flowers

Beautiful landscapes, sea, sun – Rhodes is not unique in that respect, but Rhodians regard themselves as just a little different. They believe their island is special. Even in antiquity there was a love of the monumental and grandiose. Cleobulus, one of the Seven Sages, urged his fellow islanders to exercise moderation. 'Avoid extremes' was his motto and yet, only a few centuries later, they were building one of the ancient world's grandest statues, the bronze *Colossus of Rhodes* which was one of the Seven Wonders of the Ancient World.

A popular hobby

Today Rhodes is richer and more cosmopolitan than the two other, larger islands in the eastern Mediterranean, Crete and Cyprus. For decades it has been a destination for hundreds of thousands of tourists from all over the world. Some worry that the island will become the Majorca of the Aegean and lose its distinctive charm – unspoilt landscapes, shepherds, fishermen, bright clear light on the chalky white walls – all this is still there, but visitors do have to seek it out. The 20th century has not passed Greece and Rhodes by without a trace.

Position and Size

Rhodes is the biggest of the Dodecanese Islands (*Dodekanissa* means Twelve Islands) and lies about 20km (12 miles) from the west coast of Turkey in the southeastern Aegean. The coastline extends for 220km (136 miles) and encloses an area of 1,398sq.km (540sq miles), making Rhodes the fourth biggest Greek island. In fact there are about 200 islands and islets in the Dodecanese archipelago but only about 20 of them are permanently inhabited.

Geologically, the islands are the summits of a mountain range which disappeared under the sea millions of years ago. They form the link between the Dinaric Alps and the Taurus Mountains of Asia Minor. Rhodes and Karpathos are the highest in the range, both reaching a height of 1,215m (3,985ft).

Climate

A Mediterranean climate

The west coast is windier than the east coast

Rhodes enjoys a Mediterranean climate, characterised by dry, hot summers and wet, mild winters. It lies on the same latitude as north Africa and is sheltered by the Turkish mainland, so the summers are very hot. A pleasant gentle breeze often blows but the *meltimi* north wind does not cool as much as on the Cyclades, where even in summer it can develop into a storm. Windsurfers and sailors may like to know that the west coast is windier than the east coast, and Rhodes beats even Crete or Cyprus for sunshine. Even in October, air temperatures can reach 30°C (86°F) and water temperatures 23°C (73°F). These gradually fall off from the end of October, with a low point for air temperature of around 16°C (60°F) in February.

For those who can choose when to take their holidays, May/June or September/October are the ideal times to visit Rhodes as the weather is cooler and the tourist influx has subsided. Springtime is particularly attractive when the island's flora is at its best. September and October are ideal for beach holidays. Admittedly the end of October may bring a few showers, but they are usually short and warm. Finding accommodation in October is normally not a problem. The ferry companies are still operating their summer timetables and 'island hopping' remains feasible.

The winter months are less inviting. Rainfall can be both heavy and prolonged. Most hotels close and the inter-island boat network is reduced to a minimum.

Nature and the environment

Lemons grow in abundance

Rhodes is one of the greenest and most fertile of the Greek islands. The abundance and variety of its flora is attributable to the southerly latitude and the mild Mediterranean climate. Of course, plants of European origin flourish here, but many Asian and North African species thrive too. There are several hundred plant species which can only be found in Greece and 27 of them occur on Rhodes, including the yellowy-white flowered Rhodian peony (*paeonia rhodia*) and the yellow fritillary (*fritillaria rhodia*).

Varieties of orchid such as the butterfly orchid, tongue orchid and bug orchid can often be seen in the undergrowth of the light pine forests or along the footpaths. The yellow horned poppy and dwarf edelweiss can be found near sandy beaches, while the pearly everlasting flower and the bird's foot trefoil are sometimes found by rocky shores.

The strawberry tree is a pretty sight and is typical of Rhodes and the whole eastern Mediterranean basin. Its white and sometimes pink flowers produce red or orange berries which taste like strawberries. The sweet, floury fruit can be eaten but it is not rich in flavour. One unusual plant – a native of Asia – which only grows in the Valley of the Butterflies (*see page 49*) is the oriental amber (*liquidambar orientalis*) or sweet gum tree.

At higher altitudes the vegetation consists of low-growing thorn bushes or *phrygana*, a combination of plants such as kermes oaks, globe thistles, broom, cistus and a number of flowering plants including varieties of iris. Extravagantly colourful bougainvillea, oleander and pomegranate trees grow everywhere on Rhodes, but no roses. Botanically speaking at least, there is no justification for the name 'Rose Island'.

The Italians, who occupied the island from 1911 to 1943, are credited with planting the wide expanses of forest, but unfortunately many acres of woodland are lost due to forest fires. These, along with poachers, have in turn threatened the survival of the island's deer and as a result a conservation group called the Platoni Society was founded in 1994. In comparison to the rest of Europe, Greek woodland has fared well, with acid rain only affecting 18 percent of tree stocks.

Woodland

Population

Rhodes is one of the few islands where the population has declined over recent decades. The present number is about 100,000, of which some 55,000 live in Rhodes City. The population of the ancient commercial port was double this size.

The remaining 45,000 islanders are spread around the other 41 villages and 60 tiny settlements on the island with Archangelos and its 3,500 inhabitants the second largest. In Rhodes City lives a Turkish minority of about 2,000, all of whom are now Greek citizens, and the two communities live in harmony. The Jewish community numbered about 2,000 until 1944 but now there are said to be only seven families left (*see page 31*).

Rhodians have never been poor and today they rank as one of the most prosperous sectors of Greek society. Life expectancy on Rhodes averages out at 78. Men can expect to live to 76 and women to 80. They regard themselves as a cosmopolitan people and a look back at their history will explain why that is so. Many of them have relatives in the USA, Australia and other European countries. They are generally very welcoming to foreigners and it is easy to make contact but they are much more likely to invite you for a coffee in a café or supper in a *taverna* than into their homes.

Greeks and Turks live side by side

Ready for the summer crush

Admiring the Temple of Athena

Wine production is a traditional industry

Economy

Tourism is the main source of income for Rhodians. The tourist industry first became established here in the early 1960s and now more than two thirds of the population depend on it for their livelihood. About 13 percent of Greek tourists (131,000) head for Rhodes and in 1992, a record year, the number of visitors exceeded the one million mark. German tourists top the list (229,000) with British holidaymakers (191,000) not far behind. Italians (60,000) and Swedes (54,000) also enjoy the island. This was an improvement of 24 percent on the 1991 figure. In 1993 alone, the number of hotel beds rose by 5,000.

Income from agriculture has been declining although the climate and the irrigation system adopted from Israel make it possible for more than one harvest per year. The only exceptions to this trend are wine production and the export of olives – two traditional industries. Fewer islanders make their living from fishing now. The sea around Rhodes is not good fishing ground and, fish are an expensive delicacy. Altogether, the Greek economy is in a poor state and annual inflation runs at around 15 percent.

Administration

The free elections of 17 November 1974 saw the foundation of the Greek democratic state (*Elliniki Demokratia Ellas*). The president is elected by parliament for a five-year term. Parliament has 300 members all elected by universal suffrage for a four-year term. Rhodes City is the administrative centre for the Dodecanese Islands. The mayor is a PASOK member (Panhellenic Socialist Movement) and in the elections of 10 October 1993 he won 65 percent of the Rhodian vote.

Bureaucracy, corruption and nepotism have tainted Greek politics for many years and, despite the emergence of some new political groupings, the two-party system still prevails. It is difficult to see any dramatic changes in the near future. Nevertheless, current affairs is *the* topic of conversation in the cafés and no one could ever accuse the Greek people of political apathy.

Language

Ancient Greek has been subjected to a variety of influences in the transition to the language of modern Greece. Many Turkish, Italian and French words have found their way into the vocabulary.

In 1830, soon after the modern Greek state was founded, the government decided to create a language. It was felt that the everyday language (*dhemotiki*) was too common and so an artificial language more akin to ancient Greek (*katharevousa*) was adopted as the official language. In the words of Lawrence Durrell, 'to the average peasant it was no more comprehensible than sanskrit' and the majority of the population had to learn it as if it were a foreign language. The government of Andreas Papandreou finally abolished the use of *katharevousa* as the language of officialdom, in favour of *dhemotiki*, which was also simplified. All street and road signs are now written in the Latin alphabet.

English is Rhodes second language followed by French. Older Greek people may know some Italian. German is spoken by many Greeks: over one tenth of the population has at some time lived in Germany as 'guest workers'. But, learning a few Greek phrases will help, especially if you intend to visit some of the remote parts of the island.

Gestures and facial expressions often have different meanings. The best example and one that can lead to many misunderstandings is the nod of the head. An affirmative nod for us means 'no' to Greeks.

Kimisis Theotokou in Salakos

Religion and Customs

The vast majority of Greeks belong to the Greek Orthodox Church. Tradition and customs are closely linked with the Church because without it, it is unlikely that the Greek nation would have survived Turkish domination and still retained its own language, culture and traditions. The Orthodox Church was never banned as Islam tolerates the existence of other religions. A small minority of about 2,000 Moslems live on Rhodes. The Church approved the War of Independence opposing Turkish rule in 1821. Against this background it is not surprising that religion assumes an important part in the life of many Greeks.

Icons (*see page 69*) occupy a central part not only in church services but also in homes and workplaces. Bus and taxi drivers often attach brightly-coloured pictures of saints to their windscreens.

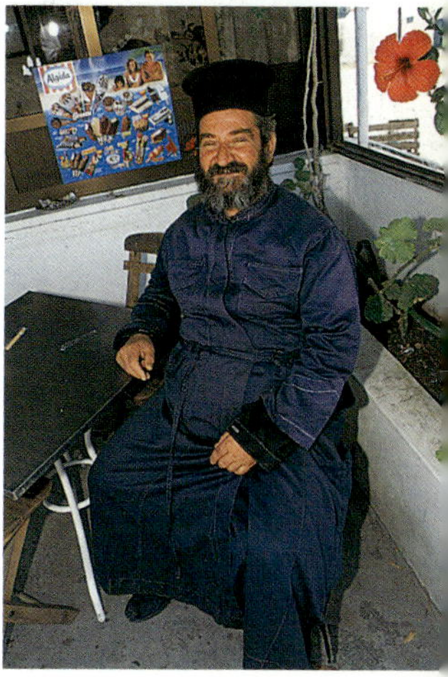

Orthodox priest

Historical Highlights

c 4000BC The first human settlements established on the island.

1600BC Rhodes' Mycenean period; settlement by the Achaians, who found the first cities of Lindos, Kamiros and Ialyssos.

15th–14th century BC Cretan Minoans found trading colonies on the west coast.

12th century BC According to Homer, Rhodes contributed nine ships to the Trojan War.

1100BC Beginning of the Dorian migration. The Dorians divide the island into three regions with capitals in Lindos, Kamiros and Ialyssos.

8th century BC The three city states founded by the Dorians create a strong naval force. They combine with Kos, Knidos and Halicarnassus to form the Dodecanese Hexapolis (six city league).

650BC First Rhodian colonies on Sicily, and in Italy, Spain and France.

c 550BC Cleobulus, one of the Seven Sages, rules in Lindos.

490–479BC In the Persian Wars the Rhodians fight alongside the Persians, but after defeat in 478 join the Delian League under the leadership of Athens.

408BC Amalgamation (*synoikismos*) of the three city states to create a new capital, Rhodes City, which quickly becomes an important trading centre. Period of cultural and economic ascendancy.

336BC Alexander the Great of Macedonia occupies Kos. Rhodes joins him against Persia.

331BC Founding of Alexandria, Egypt, which becomes an important trading partner.

323BC Alexander's generals divide up the conquered areas, leading to war. Rhodes allies with Egypt for economic reasons.

305–304BC The Macedonian Demetrios Poliorketes, the feared 'Besieger of Cities', fails to capture Rhodes despite the latest military equipment. Chares of Lindos is said to have completed the '*Colossus of Rhodes*' within 12 years (304–292BC) in honour of Helios, the sun god.

304BC Rhodes establishes first relations with Rome, and continues to thrive as a commercial port and important naval power until 166BC when Rome declared Delos a free port.

227BC Earthquake. The island is devastated and the Colossus demolished.

201BC Philip of Macedonia occupies Rhodian possessions in Asia Minor. Rhodes calls on Rome for assistance.

191BC Rhodian navy joins Rome to fight against the Seleucid Antiochus II. It defeats the Syrian fleet led by Hannibal. Rome rewards Rhodes with territory in Asia Minor.

171–168BC During the third Macedonian war, Rhodes takes sides with Perseus, the Macedonian king. After the defeat of the Macedonians, Rhodes relinquishes territory in Asia Minor.

164BC Alliance pact with Rome establishes a more dependent position for the island.

1st century BC As the Rhodians refuse to support Cassius in his struggle with Octavian, later to become Caesar Augustus, Cassius attacks and plunders the island. Under Augustus, Rhodes becomes a Roman province and a place of exile.

AD51 Paul lands at Lindos and begins to convert the island to Christianity.

155 A severe earthquake devastates large areas of the island.

269 Goths plunder Rhodes.

385 The Bishop of Rhodes becomes a Metropolitan with responsibility for Samos, Chios, Kos and the main islands of the Cyclades.

395 With the partition of the Roman Empire, Rhodes becomes part of the eastern provinces with Byzantium as its capital. For a short time during Byzantine rule, the island is occupied by Arabs.

7th–8th century Saracens attack the island.

1082 The Venetians establish a trading post on Rhodes.

1096–9 First Crusade. Crusaders make Rhodes a supply base on their way to the Holy Land.

1204 After the defeat of Constantinople by the Franks in the 4th Crusade, the Byzantine governor, Leon Gavalas, appoints himself ruler of Rhodes.

1261 Rhodes becomes a part of the Byzantine Empire again, but is administered in effect by the Genoese who conquered it in 1248.

1306 After the loss of their base in the Holy Land to the Mamluks (1187), the Knights of St John (*see below*) come to an agreement with the Genoan Vignolo di Vignoli over the occupation of Rhodes, Kos and Leros.

1309–1522 The Knights of St John acquire control of the whole island. In 1480, they resist a 90-day siege by Sultan Mehmet II but in 1522 they succumb to attacks lasting six months by Suleyman the Magnificent.

1523–1912 Turkish domination. No Greeks allowed inside the capital city after nightfall. The 1821 War of Independence against Turkish rule slowly spreads to Rhodes and the other Dodecanese Islands.

1911–12 Italian-Turkish War. The Lausanne Treaty of 18 October 1912 results in Rhodes and the other Dodecanese islands passing into Italian control. They become the Isole Italiane dell' Egeo until 1943.

1939 World War II begins.

1943–5 German troops occupy Rhodes after the fall of Mussolini.

1945 British troops liberate the island.

1945–7 British Transitional Government. In February 1947 at the Paris Peace Conference, Italy secedes Rhodes and the Dodecanese Islands to Greece.

1967–74 Military dictatorship in Greece.

1974 A large part of the Turkish minority leaves the island during the Cyprus crisis.

1974–81 The conservative Nea Demokratia party takes control. In 1981, Greece becomes the 10th member of the European Community. The left-wing PASOK party wins the election and Andreas Papandreou becomes president.

1988 Heads of State and political leaders of the European Community gather on Rhodes for a summit meeting.

1990–3 Konstantin Mitsotakis wins the 1990 election for the Nea Demokratia party.

1993 The socialist PASOK party under Andreas Papandreou wins elections on 10 October 1993.

The Knights of St John

The Knights of the Order of St John of Jerusalem held sway in Rhodes from 1309 to 1522. The Knights Hospitallers, as they are sometimes called, were founded in 1070 by a group of Italian merchants in Amalfi to care for the sick, train doctors, protect pilgrims and wage war on the infidel. The core of the knights, about 600, originated from noble European families and were divided into seven, later eight 'tongues' or nationalities: Auvergne, France, Provence, Germany, England, Italy and Spain (later divided into Aragon and Castille). At the top of the brotherhood's hierarchy was the Grand Master who was elected for life.

They took an active part in the Crusades but, following the fall of the last Christian stronghold in Palestine, they were driven out of the Holy Land. They initially sought refuge in Cyprus but with the Pope's blessing transferred to Rhodes, officially a part of the Byzantine Empire but actually controlled by Genoese pirates. The knights built a powerful fleet of war galleys, declared themselves Guardians of the High Seas and continued to fulfil their original caring role.

In 1522, after a total of 213 years on Rhodes, they were finally ousted by the Ottoman Suleyman the Magnificent. However, the sultan treated them with dignity, allowing them and their possessions free passage off the island. They later established a new base in Malta where they became known as the Knights of Malta after Emperor Charles V granted them sovereignty of the island. The Order continues to work as a charitable organisation, caring for the sick and wounded worldwide.

Symi
Nimos
Nimborio
Symi
Symi
Pedi
616
Panormitis
Sesklio
Rhodes
Alimia
Alimia
Khalki
Khalki
Nimborio (Khalki)
Khalki
Soroni
4
5
Kamiros
Kalavarda
Agios Soulas
Salakos
Mandrikon
Kapion
Profitis Ilias
798
Dimilia
Eleousa
Apollona
Fountoukli (Ag. Nikolaos)
Castello
Kamiros Skala
Kritinia
Embona
7
Ataviros
1215
Artamitou
4
Cape Armenistis
Agios Isidoros
Laerma
Siana
Castle
Monolithos
Cape Monolithos
Thari
Istrios
Profilia
Ipseni
Lardos
Asklipio
Vathi
2
Apolakia
Arnitha
Gennadi
4
Mesanagros
MEDIT
4
Lahania
4
2
Kattavia
Ag. Pavlos
Chochlakas
Cape Lahania
Plimiri
Prasonisi
Cape Prasonisi

Cape Koumbourno
Rhodes City
Kritika
Trianda
Kremasti
Ixia
Ialysos (Trianda)
Paradisi
Damatria
Pastida
Theologos
Cape Vodi
Koskinou
Baths of Kalithea
Maritsa
Petaloudes
Eleousa
Faliraki
Kalithies
Cape Ladiko
Psinthos
Afandou
Archipolis
Kolymbia
Epta Piges
Tsambika
Arhangelos
Malona
Profitis Ilias
512
Cape Arhangelos
Masari
Feraklos
Haraki
Kalathos
Acropolis
Lindos
Pefka
ERRANEAN SEA
N
ROUTES 1–7
0
10 km

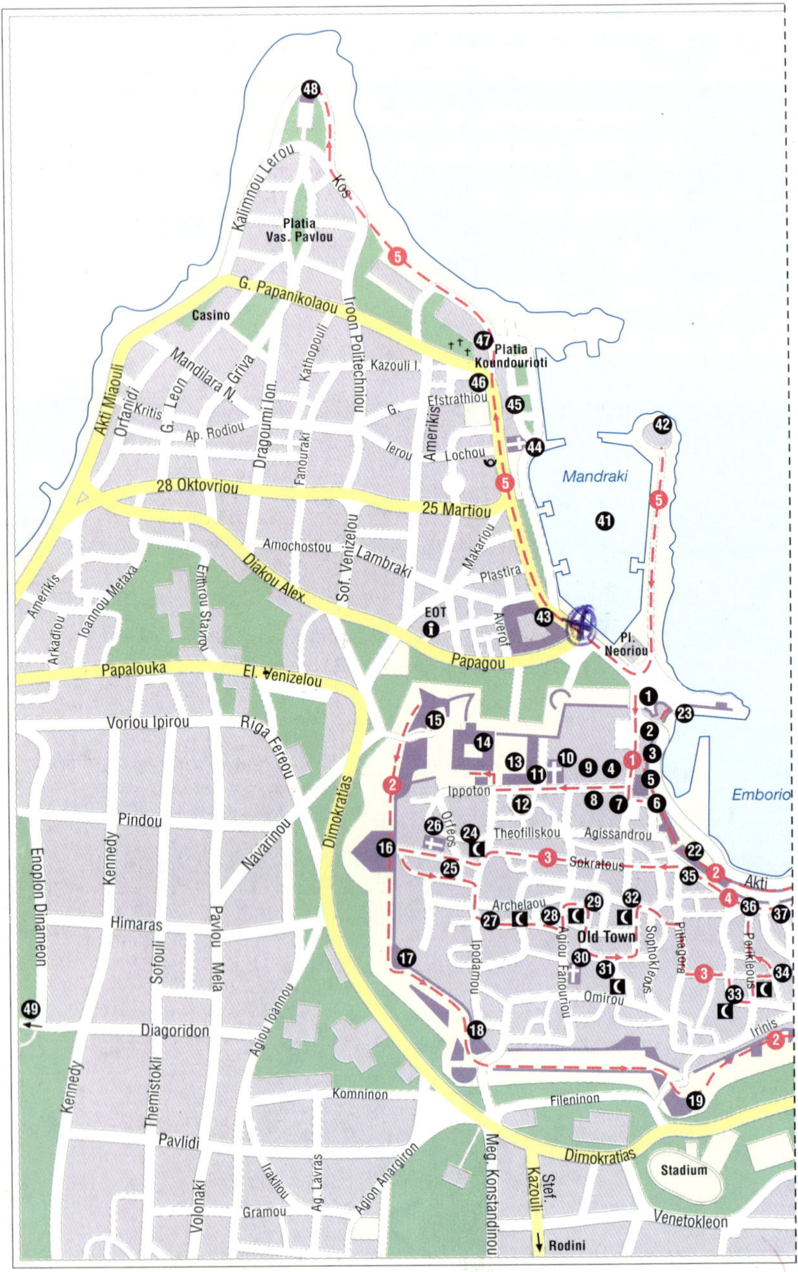

Platia
Vas. Pavlou
Kalimnou Lerou
Kos
G. Papanikolaou
Casino
Iroon Politechniou
Platia
Koundourioti
Kazouli I.
Kathopouli
Mandilara N.
Griva
Akti Miaouli
Orfanidi
Kritis
G. Leon
Ap. Rodiou
Dragoumi Ion.
Fanouraki
G.
Ierou
Efstrathiou
Amerikis
Lochou
Mandraki
28 Oktovriou
25 Martiou
Amochostou
Lambraki
Sof. Venizelou
Makariou
Plastira
Diakou Alex.
Erithrou Stavrou
Ioannou Metaxa
Amerikis
Arkadiou
EOT
Averof
Papagou
Pl.
Neoriou
Papalouka
El. Venizelou
Voriou Ipirou
Riga Fereou
Ippoton
Emborio
Theofiliskou
Agissandrou
Orfeos
Sokratous
Akti
Pindou
Navarinou
Dimokratias
Enoplon Dinameon
Kennedy
Himaras
Archelaou
Old Town
Ipodamou
Agiou Fanouriou
Sophokleous
Pithagora
Perikleous
Omirou
Sofouli
Pavlou
Mela
Diagoridon
Agiou Ioannou
Irinis
Kennedy
Themistokli
Komninon
Fileninon
Pavlidi
Dimokratias
Stadium
Meg. Konstandinou
Stef.
Kazouli
Iraklion
Ag. Lavras
Agion Anargiron
Volonaki
Gramou
Venetokleon
Rodini

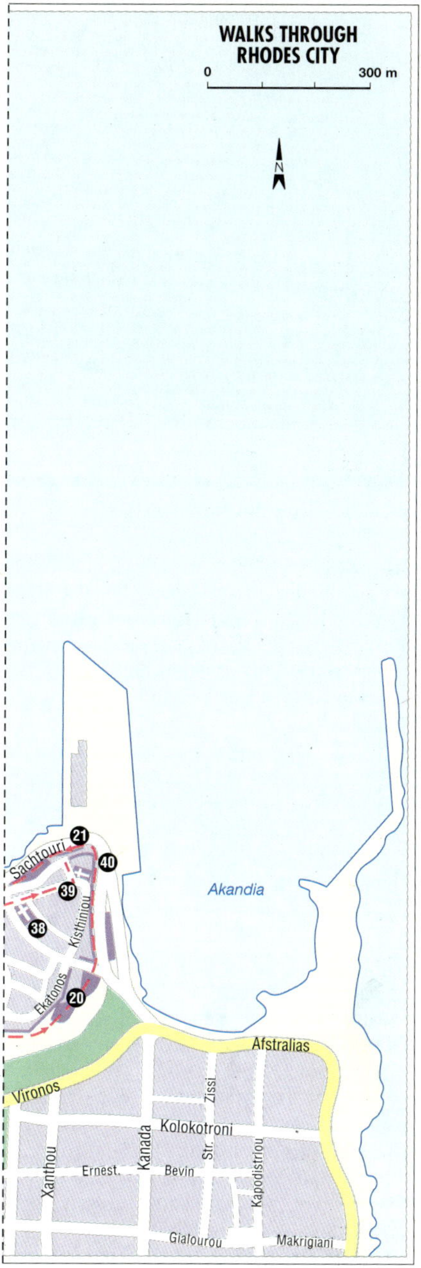

Rhodes City Plan

1. Liberty Gate (Pili Eleftherias)
2. Temple of Aphrodite
3. Inn of Auvergne
4. Hospital of the Old Knights
5. Byzantine Museum
6. Inn of England
7. Hospital of the New Knights
8. Street of the Knights
9. Inn of Italy
10. Inn of France
11. Agia Trias Chapel
12. Inn of Spain
13. Inn of Provence
14. Palace of the Grand Masters
15. Amboise Gate
16. St George's Gate
17. Tower of Spain
18. St Mary's Tower
19. Agios Ioannis Gate
20. Del Carretto Tower
21. St Catherine's Gate
22. Thalassini Gate
23. Arsenal Gate
24. Mosque of Suleyman
25. Turkish Library
26. Church of Agios Georgios
27. Mustafa Pasha Baths
28. Mustafa Pasha Mosque
29. Kavakli Mosque (Agios Spiridon Church)
30. Basilica of Agios Fanourios
31. Rejeb Pasha Mosque
32. Demirli Mosque
33. Dolapli Mosque (Agias Trias Church)
34. Ilk Mihrab Mosque (Agia Ekaterini Church)
35. Kastellania
36. Archbishop's Palace/Admiralty Building
37. Kal de Shalom Synagogue
38. Panagia Kastrou Church
39. Hospital of St Catherine
40. Agios Panteleimon Church
41. Mandraki Harbour
42. St Nicholas Fort
43. Nea Agora
44. Evangelismos Church
45. Governor's Palace
46. National Theatre
47. Turkish Cemetery
48. Aquarium
49. Acropolis Hill

Street of the Knights
Preceding pages: west coast cove; stag at the Mandraki harbour

Route 1

★★ Rhodes City – Six walks through Rhodes

The island's main town, Rhodes (pop. 55,000), is ideally suited for those who want to spend their days sunbathing or indulging in sports activities and their evenings enjoying the nightlife. For those who want a more relaxing holiday, then one of the resorts further south is probably a better choice, but try to allow at least two full days for a tour of the town and environs.

Rhodes City divides neatly into two. There is the old walled city where antiquity, the Orient and the Occident merge and which boasts a history stretching back thousands of years. And then there is the new town with its beaches, bars and discos, a magnet for the many thousands of young holidaymakers.

Holidaymakers in the old town

History

Rhodes is regarded as one of the most important cities of antiquity. Alongside Alexandria, it was once the centre of the Hellenistic world. The results of the latest research were revealed at an archaeological conference in Rhodes in 1993 and it is clear that the founding fathers of this once huge city, the surface area of which exceeded that of Classical Athens, were town planners with vision.

This rich trading centre dating from 408BC was the first city to set aside a quarter of the available land for further development. The open spaces were used as gardens until the 3rd century BC, when a massive population influx made new building work necessary. The street plan of Rhodes resembled that of Piraeus, which the famous architect Hippodamos from Miletus laid out, although the network of streets was much denser and the roads wider – testimony to the prosperity of this flourishing commercial centre.

Another recent discovery is the narrowness of the city walls. As the city with its five harbours could not be protected easily from potential invaders, the military strategists succeeded in creating the impression that a strong fortified wall existed. High walls with towers were built, but they were only 60cm (2ft) thick, by far the thinnest city walls of any ancient town. Even the so-called 'Besieger of Cities', Demetrios Poliorketes, fell into the trap. In 305BC, equipped with the latest military hardware, he was unable to conquer Rhodes. As a token of gratitude for having narrowly escaped defeat, the Rhodians erected a bronze statue of the sun god Helios – soon to win admiration as one of the Seven Wonders of the Ancient World. A little later on, a new, thicker wall was built. This has only been uncovered in recent years, but the 4-m (13-ft) thick wall, towers and ditches are a fine example of early Hellenistic fortifications.

In the following centuries, Rhodes tried to pursue a policy of diplomacy whenever possible and agreed to a string of different alliances. They joined forces first with the Persians, followed by the Athenians, the Romans, the Macedonians and finally the Romans again and this at a time when Rome's dominion extended over Rhodes and the whole of Greece.

For the next 2,000 years the fate of the island was to be determined by foreign powers. During Byzantine rule Rhodes was remote from the levers of power. Under the Ottomans it was cut off from Europe. Only in the interim period did the island really flourish. In 1309, the Crusader Knights of St John landed on the island. But at the beginning of the 16th century, as the result of a 'gentleman's agreement' with the Turks, the knights withdrew and decline set in (*see page 11*).

Situated on the dividing line between the Occident and the Orient, Rhodes has incorporated a mixture of the two cultures –an important element in the island's charm.

The city walls

Palace of the Grand Masters

Walk 1

The ★★ Old Town – the Middle Ages come alive

The Palace of the Grand Masters with its turrets, towers and huge walls dominates the old town, itself surrounded by a 4-km (2½-mile) wall. During the Middle Ages, the town was divided into two parts. The northern section of the Old Town, the fortress or *collachium,* was used by the knights, where they were well shielded from the indigenous population who lived in the southern commercial section. In this way the knights, who were committed to a vow of chastity, could be kept away from the temptations of worldly life, or more precisely, from the pretty Greek women.

The Italians are responsible for the way the Old Town looks today: in 1920, the occupying forces commissioned del Fausto, an architect, to rebuild it as the knights had left it in 1523, using old plans and engravings. However, the unfettered enthusiasm of the Italian builders did lead to overstatement and the Palace of the Grand Masters has been the subject of fierce criticism.

In the interior, the builders have clearly deviated from the original, devouring huge amounts of money in the process. It is assumed that the Italians did not shy away from incurring heavy costs because the palace was intended for use as a summer residence by Mussolini and the Italian king, Victor Emmanuel II. The Street of the Knights (Ippoton), however, was restored much more sensitively and with great care, which included the removal of the wooden balconies installed by the Turks so that the ladies of the harem could keep an eye on the street activities. It is now the finest and most interesting part of the Old Town with a unity and compactness which are unique in Europe.

Son and shades

The best times to walk through the Old Town are in the morning when most tourists are sunning themselves on the beach, and then again in the early evening or at night, when it is easy to travel back 500 years in time and understand the appeal of this beautiful area .

A walk through the 'town within a town' will last about an hour, not including time spent in the museums.

The Temple of Aphrodite

The walk begins at the **Liberty Gate** (Pili Eleftherias) ❶ which was knocked out of the enormous city wall in 1924 to give easier access into the Old Town. This is the only part of the wall that has been altered to improve the flow of traffic. The gate opens on to the **Plateia Simi** (or Arsenal Square). The 3rd century BC foundations of the **Temple of Aphrodite** ❷ in the centre of the square seem a little out of place amid the late medieval architecture of the Crusaders. Other ancient remains, columns and a Hellenistic street have been uncovered behind the bank.

The **Municipal Art Gallery** is housed in the bank and it is one of the few places outside Athens where 20th-century Greek art is displayed. The 300 or so works include paintings by such famous artists as Tsarouchis, Moralis, Semertzidis and Theofilos, the famous Greek naive artist from the island of Lesbos.

Inn of Auvergne

Crusader buildings can be found on the adjoining ★ **Argirokastrou Square** (Plateia Argirokastrou). On the east side stands the ★ **Inn of Auvergne** ❸. This was com-

Old Knights' Hospital

pleted in 1507 by Guy de Blanchefort, one of the Grand Masters. His coat of arms and the year of completion are shown above the Gothic portal arch. A loggia facing onto the street and a flight of steps to the side give the building some of the elegance of a Venetian palace.

The ★ **Old Knights' Hospital** ❹ opposite is 50 years older and the work of another Grand Master, Roger de Pins. When the new, larger hospital was built, it was used as an armoury, hence it is still referred to as the Palazzo dell' Armeria. It is now used by the Archaeological Service of the Dodecanese Islands. The southern wing is occupied by the ★ **Museum of Decorative Arts** where furniture, costumes, embroidery and pottery from the Dodecanese Islands are displayed. In the middle of the square, the Italian architects placed an early Christian baptismal font and a monolith brought here from the Agia Irini church near Apolakia. It fits in well with the simplicity of the Crusader buildings.

Pottery exhibit in the Museum of Decorative Arts

Situated a few yards further south on the Plateia Moussiou are two other interesting museums: the **Byzantine Museum** ❺ in the ★ **Mitropolis** (Panagia tou Kastro) which the Crusaders converted into a late Gothic-style church and the Archaeological Museum in the New Knights' Hospital. Its entrance faces the **Inn of England** ❻ which dates from 1483. It was completely destroyed in the 19th century and then rebuilt by the Italians in 1919.

The ★ **New Knights' Hospital** ❼ is as impressive as the Palace of the Grand Masters and there are similarities in style. It was started in 1440 by Jean Bonpart de Lastic, but the money ran out and it was finally completed in 1489 by Pierre d'Aubusson. Above the entrance stands a bas-relief with two angels who hold de Lastic's coat of arms in their hands. The Infirmary Hall is on the first floor. Some 50m (160ft) in length, over 12m (40ft) wide and 7m (23ft) high, it could accommodate up to 100 beds during a siege.

Archaeological Museum

In times of peace, invalids from all over Europe came here for treatment. An altar where mass could be performed for the dead once stood in the three-sided, apse-like bay above the portal. The impressive two-storey arcades surrounding the inner courtyard offered some welcome shade and a staircase without a bannister opened on to the upper floor.

The former hospital now houses the ★★ **Archaeological Museum** (Tuesday to Thursday, 8.30am–3pm) with exhibits dating from the Mycenaean period right through to late Hellenistic times, including statues, funerary steles, pottery (vases, amphoras, bowls and pots), jewellery mainly from the necropoles at Ialysos and Kamiros and also a collection of coins. It is difficult to imagine the treasures that would be displayed if the Romans had not carried off so many of the magnificent works of art that fell into their hands.

The Small Aphrodite

Of particular note are the two Aphrodites, especially the exquisite 'kneeling' statue which is sometimes referred to as the *Small Aphrodite*. Created around 100BC, this 49-cm (19-in) figure in an almost translucent alabaster is a delightful piece. The smooth marble emphasises the dainty features of the remarkably cold, almost distant figure who sits in an unnatural pose, either tying up or loosening her hair. It's not known who carved this statue.

The other Aphrodite, the moving *Venus Pudica* or the *Modest Aphrodite,* is so called because she has not entirely allowed her robe to fall. This oversized statue is a masterpiece from the 4th century BC, a period noted as the heyday of Rhodian sculpture. For many centuries it lay on the sea bed, but in 1929 it was discovered and rescued by fishermen. Although eroded and misshapen by the seawater, it still retains its simple beauty, calm detached dignity and a timeless perfection.

Mopping up at the Archaeological Museum

Another of the museum's attractions is the monumental head of Helios (c 150BC). The holes at the rear to which the golden halo was attached are proof that this is the head of the young sun god. The sad dreamy face, the slightly open mouth and curly hair match the features shown on many older coins. The model for this head was probably the Colossus.

Krito and Timarista

The funerary stele of Krito and Timarista which was found in Kamiros is one of the most important pieces of sculpture from Rhodes' Classical period. This 2-m (6-ft) high relief which dates from the 5th century BC depicts mother and daughter bidding each other farewell. The despairing Krito lays her hand tenderly on her mother Timarista who, as is clear from the position of her legs, is on the point of leaving this world for good. The two *kouroi* (youth figures) originated from Paros and Naxos and date from around the same time.

Exploring the Street of the Knights

An important collection of vases and *objets d'art* are to be found in the rooms in the north, south and west. Other artistic objects from the Crusader years – coats of arms and tomb carvings – are displayed in the Infirmary Hall.

★★ **Street of the Knights** (Ippoton) ❽. This late Gothic street follows the course of the ancient road which once led from the harbour to the Temple of Helios, the present site of the Palace of the Grand Masters. On either side of the narrow lane stand the inns of the 'Seven Tongues' (nationalities), which later became eight, and other buildings from the Crusader years. To which nationality each inn belonged can be determined by the coat of arms attached to the simple facade. The year of completion is also shown and all date from the 14th or 15th century. Although many are now occupied by offices, archaeological institutes and galleries, do not be afraid to step inside and take a look at the inner courtyards or the small but thriving gardens and roof gardens – a luxury appreciated by the knights who favoured the pleasures of earthly pursuits.

The Inn of France

The first corner house on the right-hand side facing the New Knights' Hospital is the ★ **Inn of Italy** ❾ built as late as 1519 by Fabrizio del Carretto. It is the only inn apart from the English one that has been fully rebuilt. The French formed by far the biggest contingent of the Rhodian knights and the finest building is almost certainly the ★ **Inn of France** ❿. The year 1492 can be read above the pointed arch of the main entrance and alongside stands the coat of arms of Emery d'Amboise. Between the middle windows on the first floor is the French fleur-de-lys.

The elegant building situated in the narrow alley which branches off to the right was also part of the French hostel and is known as the **Zizim House**. Zizim was the brother of Sultan Bayazet and as he was supposedly the

Palace of the Grand Masters with detail of sculpture

first-born, he had a claim to the throne. The knights granted him asylum in the same way that they offered succour to many other victims of political persecution. However, Zizim proved to be rather an awkward guest. The French could cope with his bad table manners, but not the political consequences of their hospitality. They convinced him that he would do better to make his case in France, but once there, Bayazet removed his fraternal opponent in a way quite normal for those days. Zizim was poisoned.

The street continues with the **Agia Trias Chapel** ⓫, probably commissioned by Grand Master Raymond Béranger in the 14th century for the French knights, the ★ **Inn of Spain** ⓬, the **Inn of Provence** ⓭ and the loggia of St John of which only a few ruined columns remain. To the left stood the Church of St John where the grand masters found their last resting place. Like the loggia and the Palace of the Grand Masters it was razed to the ground in 1856 when the Turkish magazine exploded.

Palace of the Grand Masters

The ★ **Palace of the Grand Masters** (daily except Monday, fortress, 8.30am–3pm; museum, 10am–3pm) ⓮ which dominates the Mandraki Harbour and all of the Old Town was built by the Crusader knights in the middle of the 14th century. Ostensibly a free-standing fortress, it was linked by tunnels to the city walls. The present building is a reconstruction, completed in 1939 by Mario de Vecchi, the then governor of the Dodecanese Islands. While the Italian architects ensured that external walls were faithfully reconstructed in accordance with old drawings and engravings, they gave free rein to their fantasies when rebuilding and furnishing the interior. It does very little to enlighten visitors about the knights' 200-year dominion. Nevertheless, a visit to the fortress is worth the effort if only for the marvellous Roman and early Christian ★★ **floor mosaics** which the Italians brought over from the neighbouring island of Kos.

In 1993, to commemorate 2,400 years of Rhodes City, a ★★ **permanent exhibition** of archaeological finds from the last three decades was opened on the ground floor of the palace. The collection, which should really be seen in conjunction with the works of art in the Archaeological Museum, is arranged in themes. About a thousand exhibits illustrate such topics as *Feasts and Banquets* and *Shrines and Idols*. Many of the rooms offer superb ★ **views** over the town, the fortifications and the sea.

Behind the fortress is the Odhos Orfeos where artists, most of whom are art students, will produce an amazingly accurate portrait in about an hour.

An artist at work

Walk 2

★★ The City Walls

The city walls are only accessible on two days of the week (Tuesday and Saturday at 2.45pm). The walk of about an hour begins at the Palace of the Grand Masters and ends by the Arsenal Gate at the Emborio Harbour. It is possible to walk round the outside of the walls, and from the Old Town there are plenty of opportunities to see parts of the wall and the gates.

Rhodes City's huge and ingeniously built structure is a unique example of medieval defensive fortifications. At the time of the Crusaders, it was regarded as the best-laid defensive system in the whole of Europe. The fortifications do not just consist of a simple ring wall, but include ramparts, a double ditch, staggered towers, bastions and gates which form a complex, almost impenetrable, labyrinth. No invading army ever captured Rhodes, not even Suleyman the Magnificent.

So how did the Turks win control of the city? Some think the grand master was betrayed. Perhaps the knights ran out of ammunition. The most probable explanation is that the knights could not resist the overwhelming superiority of the Turks and conceded. It is said that the 7,500 defenders faced an army of 60,000 Turks.

After their arrival in Rhodes at the beginning of the 14th century, the Knights of St John improved and modernised the Byzantine defences, but after an assault by Sultan Mehmet II in 1480 which almost ended in defeat, the fortifications were rebuilt. In the meantime, weaponry had advanced and the walls had to withstand the greater power of gunpowder artillery, so the knights called in the best architects and engineers from France and Italy for the job.

The City Wall walk

Amboise Gate

Thousands of Muslim slaves who had been captured by the knights in their guise as Guardians of the High Seas and then transported back to Rhodes supplied the labour and the thickness of the walls was doubled, sometimes trebled, with some sections ending up 12m (39ft) wide. The ditches were deepened and the ramparts were broadened. Round towers replaced square ones and the gates and bastions were fortified. Each of the eight 'tongues' was given a section of wall, which they were responsible for maintaining and defending. Apart from a few improvements, the walls are the same now as they were in 1523, remaining largely untouched during the 400 years of Turkish reign.

The 4-km (2½-mile) tour of the fortified walls begins at the ★ **Amboise Gate** ⓯ which was built in 1512 under the regency of Emery d'Amboise (1505–12). As it secured direct access to the Palace of the Grand Masters it had to be very well fortified. Outside the gate sporting the d'Amboise coat of arms lies a double defensive ditch which is spanned by a triple-arched bridge. Deer graze peacefully there now amid countless stone cannonballs. A third ditch runs alongside the palace wall.

The section of wall between the Amboise Gate and ★ **St George's Gate** (Agios Georgios) ⓰ used to be defended by German knights.

On the west side of the gate stands a marvellous bas-relief of St George's struggle with the dragon and just beneath it is the coat of arms of Antoine Fluvian, who was the ruling grand master (1421–37) when the gate and bastion were constructed. The next stretch as far as the ★ **Tower of Spain** ⓱ was built by Pierre d'Aubusson in 1489 and defended by the knights of Auvergne. D'Aubusson was responsible for building a major part of the wall and his coat of arms can be found at 50 different places.

Local sightseers

The three windmills

The knights of Spain were entrusted with the section of wall as far as the ★ **Agios Athanasios Gate** near ★ **St Mary's Tower** (Panagia) ⓲. It was through this gate that the young Suleyman walked as the conqueror of Rhodes in 1522. So that no other should pass through it, he ordered it to be filled in and it was not re-opened until the Italian era. English knights were entrusted with the section of wall between the Athanasios and the ★ **Agios Ioannis Gate** ⓳ – also known as the Koskinou Gate because the road to the village of Koskinou left Rhodes via this exit. The gate takes its name from the relief on the portal which shows John the Baptist. From here to the Tower of Italy, named after the Grand Master Fabrizio del Carretto (1513–21), was the responsibility of the knights of Provence and the Italians protected the wall from the ★ **Del Carretto Tower** ⓴ to ★ **St Catherine's Gate** ㉑. The harbour here still retains three of the original 13 **windmills**. The finest tower,

tower, flanked by two imposing round towers, is the ⋆ **Thalassini or Marine Gate** ㉒ which stands more or less in the middle of the Emborio Harbour, the old military harbour. Above the tower arch and the three coats of arms, an extremely life-like relief shows the Virgin Mary between Peter and John the Baptist. The section of wall facing the harbour as far as the **Arsenal Gate** ㉓ was defended by the knights of Castille.

The Marine Gate

Walk 3

The ⋆⋆ Turkish Quarter – oriental bazaar and some quiet squares

A crooked alley

The Crusaders' Old Town is undoubtedly the main attraction of Rhodes City, yet the **Turkish Quarter** is more than just a pretty appendage. The authorities have finally agreed with that view after many years of only considering buildings from Classical antiquity worthy of preservation. The Italians demolished a large number of the typically Turkish wooden balconies and what has survived is now being carefully restored, including several mosques and the many washing fountains which bear weathered Arabic inscriptions.

Preserving the houses is a priority and owners are given financial inducements to modernise their homes in keeping with the face of the Old Town. Rhodes City's Archaeological Service is charged with the task of preserving the captivating ambience of the crooked alleys and archways. The tangled layout of narrow lanes defies any logic and it is best to simply drift with the flow.

Only a few yards from the main tourist routes lie smaller, ancient or early Christian sites such as the St Michael Basilica at the end of Thukididou Street and the

Sandals galore

peaceful squares with cooling fountains. One pretty little spot is Plateia Dorieos – a square surrounded by several simple tavernas which are generally frequented by local people. Relax under the expansive shade of the old trees outside the Oasis Taverna.

The two-hour walk around the Turkish Quarter takes in all the public buildings from the Ottoman era and starts in Plateia Ippokratous. The Turkish Quarter's main thoroughfare, **Odhos Sokratous**, leads west from here towards the Mosque of Suleyman. The shops which line this busy street, sometimes known as the Grand Bazaar, sell everything from gold jewellery to goatskins. However, the character of the street has changed dramatically over the past few years. Sewing machinists and sandal-makers have been replaced by cheap souvenir shops, but there are still a few good quality shops to be found.

At the upper end of the Grand Bazaar stands the pink ★ **Mosque of Suleyman** (open only for prayers and services) ㉔, the biggest and last mosque to be built. The main building with its dome, dating from 1808, stands precisely at the spot where Sultan Suleyman the Magnificent ordered a mosque to be built in his name after he entered the town in 1523. The basins in the porch are used for washing.

In order to carry out the prophet's commandment of maintaining cleanliness, the Turks built baths and numerous wash basins – no Muslim would enter a mosque without performing the ritual washing ceremony and there is a fountain in almost every square in the Old Town. Many are decorated with ancient columns and capitals, others with glazed tiles, a skill that was mastered by the Turks.

Souvenir sombreros

The Mosque of Suleyman

A plane tree usually shelters every fountain, bringing a little greenery into the narrow maze of lanes and alleys.

Opposite the mosque in a romantic garden is the ★ **Turkish Library** ㉕, founded in 1794 by the wealthy Turk Ahmed Hasuf. It houses some valuable Persian and Arabic manuscripts and also a collection of Korans, written by hand on parchment.

Beneath the town wall down Odhos Apollonion on the left and just before the pink **Clock Tower** (1851) on Odhos Orfeos is the former Byzantine monastery church of ★ **Agios Georgios** ㉖, which is one of only three four-conch complexes on the island. Immediately after the Turks conquered the town in 1522, they converted the church into a mosque and **Koran school** (*Medresse Hurmale*). Suleyman did not build many mosques as all he had to do was add a minaret and washing fountains to a Christian church to make it a mosque, although more extensive work was needed inside. This is what happened to most churches. Not many new houses were necessary either, as the Greek inhabitants were forced to vacate their homes. Few alterations were made to these, apart from the addition of latticed wooden balconies which enabled the women to watch what was happening on the street below.

Islamic bath architecture was incorporated into the ★ **Mustafa Pasha Baths** (*Hamam*) (Tuesday 1–7pm, Wednesday to Saturday, 7am–7pm) ㉗ on the attractive Plateia Arionos with its plane and mimosa trees. The domed building has only recently been restored and for a small contribution, it is not only possible to see inside but to take a bath, too. Strictly segregated, the large domed hall is for men, while women must use the smaller annexes. Bathers should bring their own towels and soap. Sadly, the era of relaxing intervals of steam, sauna and massages are over and many Rhodians come here every day simply because they have no washing facilities at home. The *hamam* was probably built in 1764, the same year as the adjoining **Mustafa Pasha Mosque** ㉘.

Most of the churches which were made into mosques during the Ottoman period have now been converted back to Christian Greek Orthodox places of worship. Some are to be found in the lanes to the south of Arionos Square, once the centre of the Turkish Quarter. The old **Kavakli Mosque**, for example, is now **Agios Spiridon Church** ㉙ and another former mosque is now the domed ★ **Basilica of Agios Fanourios** ㉚, named after a saint who is revered not just on Rhodes but on Crete as well. The basilica lies sandwiched between Old Town houses in Odhos Agios Fanourios, just a few yards from the well-preserved, 16th-century ★ **Rejeb Pasha Mosque** ㉛ in Plateia Dorieos. Numerous fragments from the Byzantine and Crusader period were used in the construction of this mosque, in-

The Clock Tower

Backgammon outside the Koran school

Basilica of Agios Fanourios

cluding the columns and capitals in the main portal and the washing fountain. Richly decorated inside with Persian and Rhodian tiles, it is one of the most significant Turkish buildings on Rhodes and has just been restored. Remaining mosques that were originally Christian churches include the **Demirli Mosque** ㉜, the **Dolapli Mosque** (Agias Trias Church) ㉝ and the **Ilk Mihrab Mosque** (Agia Ekaterini Church) ㉞. To return to the Emborio Harbour take the Odhos Perikleous.

Ilk Mihrab Mosque

Walk 4

The ★ Jewish Quarter – almost forgotten

In earlier centuries, travellers were often curious as to why Rhodian mariners sometimes spoke to each other in Spanish. The reason was that about a quarter of the inhabitants were Sephardic Jews who had fled from the Spanish Inquisition in 1492 and who continued to speak in their dialect, known as Ladino or Spaniolic, for many years.

Around 1,500 Sephardic Jews were welcomed to Rhodes by the Ottoman rulers as they were people with many talents, such as doctors, printers and merchants. The Turks also valued their knowledge of the political and economic situation in Europe. One contemporary Jewish writer has claimed that the Turkish empire was a mother to the Jews like no other state on earth today.

They lived alongside the Turks within the town walls whereas the Christian Greeks were obliged to leave at night although their shops and workplaces were there. The Greeks had to live in the suburbs outside the gates or in the fields, because the Turks were mistrustful and feared their superior numbers – 20,000 Greeks as opposed to 7,000 Muslims and 1,500 Jews – nevertheless, the three

Ippokratous Square

ethnic groups managed to co-exist without serious tension.

Rhodian Jews earned their living not just from commerce but from other trades and professions. In the 19th century four of the five banks on the island were in Jewish hands and the first department store was owned by a Jewish family. Most of them were craftsmen and traders or hired themselves out as carriers or deck hands and some owned tavernas where kosher food was served. However, the decine of the Ottoman Empire led to a reduction in their intellectual influence and material prosperity.

The following walk begins amid the fountains of the popular ★ **Ippokratous Square**, a favourite meeting place for tourists. The wide steps of the former **Tribune of Commerce**, the ★ **Kastellania** ㉟, are an excellent place to sit and watch the international throng pass by. According to the date on the facade, the Knights of St John built this courthouse in 1503. One of the finest reliefs from the Crusader period can be seen above the portal: an angel bears the coat of arms of Emery d'Amboise in his left hand and the shield of the Knights of St John in his right hand. This building now houses the town's archives.

The 'sea horse' fountain

House in the Jewish Quarter

Aristoteles Street begins in Ippokratous Square and ends at a second very popular square in the southeast of the Old Town, the ★ **Plateia Martiron Evreon**, the Square of the Jewish Martyrs. In the middle, Italian architects have erected a pretty 'sea horse' fountain. Formerly known as the Archbishop's Square after the well-preserved **Archbishop's Palace** ㊱ on the northern side, it was renamed in the 1980s. Given the proximity of the harbour, many assume that this must have been the seat of the knights' admiralty. Three inscriptions and a dove in marble relief above the entrance portal reinforce the theory.

The Square of the Jewish Martyrs witnessed one of the most inhuman acts in Rhodes' long history and its new name will, it is hoped, ensure that the event is never forgotten. During the German occupation in 1943, 2,000 Jews were forced by SS officers to leave their homes in the nearby lanes. They were assembled in the square and then transported via Piraeus to concentration camps from which only 200 returned. Apparently, only seven Jewish families now remain on the island.

Hidden away behind reddish brown gates in Odhos Dosiadou, which branches off the square to the right, is the rather unprepossessing 16th-century **Kal de Shalom Synagogue** ㊲ and in the courtyard is a plaque commemorating the victims of the occupation. A member of the Jewish community keeps the synagogue open during the day and will show visitors round for a small donation. Money donated by Rhodian Jews in Israel and the USA has helped to pay for the recent redecoration of the interior and replaced the expensive liturgical vessels taken by the German forces. The small community cannot support a rabbi of its own and so a cleric from Athens or Salonica travels over to officiate at Jewish festivities. But little remains of the culture and way of life of the Rhodian Jews in this quarter of narrow alleys and decaying buildings.

Agios Panteleimon Church

A few yards from the Square of the Jewish Martyrs lie the impressive remains of **Panagia Kastrou Church** (Church of St Mary) ❸❽. This Gothic chapel was built by the Crusaders in the 14th century but is now split in half by Odhos Alchadef. Parts of the nave lie to the west, while to the east is the tripartite apse. Further east on the corner of Odhos Pindarou and Thisseos stands the former **Hospital of St Catherine** ❸❾. Also dating from the Crusader years, it was founded by Italian knights in the 14th century and was then renovated in 1516. Admirers of Byzantine architecture will appreciate the small **Agios Panteleimon Church** ❹⓿ just in front of the Ekaterini Gate. Although it dates from the 15th century, the interior has been modernised.

Walk 5

The ★ New Town – Miami Beach Aegean-style

The appearance of the new town is largely the work of the Italians whose occupation lasted from 1912 to 1943. Italian architects under the leadership of del Fausto renovated the Greek Quarter outside the town walls, which for centuries was the only place the Greeks had been allowed to live, and at the same time created a new town centre by the Mandraki Harbour, with wide streets, spacious squares and large public buildings.

The modern northern tip of the town bears the imprint of three decades of tourist development. Rows of sunbeds with parasols extend across the shingle beach. Young and old bask in the Rhodian sun or take advantage of the many sporting activities on offer. Hotels, restaurants, discotheques, bars and cafés, travel agents and all the shops which cater for tourists' needs line the anonymous streets. The restaurants with menus in five languages offer everything from Greek dishes to exotic specialities but scarcely any of the local population venture in.

Views of Mandraki Harbour

A walk of about two hours is best started at the **Mandraki Harbour** ❹❶. Mandraki is the diminutive form for the word *mandri*, which means pen. Perhaps the traders who brought sheep across to Rhodes christened it thus. But it is possible that the small harbour with boats packed closely together looked more like a sheep pen. Sailing yachts and cruise boats for Symi, Kos or Lindos all moor in the

Mandraki Harbour. The big ferries and ships dock in the neighbouring **Emborio Harbour**, the military harbour from the Crusader years. Freighters and tankers drop anchor in the adjacent **Akandia Harbour**.

Mandraki Harbour was created with a man-made mole when Rhodes City was founded in around 408BC. The Byzantines secured it with a look-out tower on the site of the **St Nicholas Fort** ㊷, which the Grand Master Philibert de Naillac, who presided here from 1396–1421, commissioned in around 1400 and which is now used as a lighthouse. The stag and doe which guard the harbour entrance are the symbols of Rhodes. For many years it was thought that the Colossus of Rhodes spanned the harbour entrance, but it now seems more likely that it stood near the Palace of the Grand Masters.

The *Colossus of Rhodes* is known to all students of antiquity as one of the Seven Wonders of the Ancient World, but surprisingly little is known about it apart from why it was built and who built it. Any reconstructions or pictures of the figure are the result of an artist's imagination, as no plans or smaller copies have ever been found. The massive 32-m (105-ft) bronze figure, erected in homage to the sun god Helios, is said to have been designed by been Chares of Lindos and was built to celebrate the end of an eight-month siege by the feared 'Besieger of Cities' Demetrios Poliorketes.

The construction of the Colossus took 12 years (294–282BC) but it was destroyed by an earthquake 65 years later. Clearly, it had great symbolic importance to the Rhodians, who at that time were enjoying considerable economic prosperity. But, apparently, when the Arabs

The stag and doe

Marine relief and sponge-seller at Mandraki Harbour

conquered Rhodes in AD653 they sold the fragments of the Colossus to the Syrians who needed 980 camels to carry it away, although this may have been something of an exaggeration. No remains have ever, it is said, been found since.

Facing the Mandraki Harbour and beneath the terraced gardens of the Palace of the Grand Masters lies the **Nea Agora** ㊸, the New Market. It was laid out by the Italians like an oriental bazaar in Moorish style. The white-washed halls surround an inner courtyard with a domed fish market in the middle and the vines and shady trees make it a good place from which to watch the hustle and bustle of a Mediterranean-style market.

Evangelismos Church with detail of fresco

Along the harbour promenade, the Odhos Eleftherias, stand a number of administrative buildings constructed by the Italians, including the Bank of Greece and the splendid ★ **General Post Office**. Diagonally opposite the Post Office stands the ★ **Evangelismos Church** ㊹, the church of the Metropolitan of Rhodes. The triple-naved Church of the Annunciation is a fairly faithful reconstruction of the Crusaders' Church of St John which stood near the Palace of the Grand Masters (*see page 24*) but was destroyed by a gunpowder explosion in 1856. The Italians rebuilt it here in 1925 following the old plans, adding the free-standing bell tower. The external structure combines neo-Romanesque and neo-Gothic styles and the interior is decorated with Byzantine-style frescoes.

The Greek Orthodox Archbishop of Rhodes lives in the adjoining building, the old **Governor's Palace** ㊺. This also dates from the Italian occupation and it mixes elements of Arabic, neo-Gothic and Venetian styles. In some ways it is reminiscent of the Doge's Palace in Venice and it is certainly one of the finest buildings from the Italian years. It was here that the ceremony for the handover of the Dodecanese Islands to Greece took place in 1947.

The Governor's Palace

Compared to the richly decorated Governor's Palace, the stern, cube-shaped **National Theatre** ❹❻ seems inappropriate in such a bright, sunny location. Facing the theatre on the corner of Odhos Papanikolaou lies one of the quietest, most idyllic spots in the town: the overgrown, abandoned ★ **Turkish Cemetery** ❹❼ with the small 16th-century ★ **Mourad Rais Mosque**, the only one to be built outside the town walls. It was named after one of Suleyman the Magnificent's admirals, Mourad Rais, who is buried here.

Mourad Rais Mosque

Many other Ottoman dignitaries, who fell from favour at the Sublime Porte in Istanbul and were exiled to the remote island of Rhodes, are buried here under the dense greenery of the huge eucalyptus trees. The dead include a Persian shah, several Tartar princes, a governor, an Egyptian poet and a Turkish grand vizier. In accordance with Turkish/Islamic tradition, the men's gravestones are crowned with a turban, while the women's headstones bear flower, bird and tree of life motifs.

Between 1945 and 1947, the English novelist Lawrence Durrell lived in a little house in the cemetery known as Villa Kleoboulos. He spent many years in Greece, two of them on Rhodes as a British press attaché. In his book *Reflections on a Marine Venus* he describes the landscape and the people, their culture and their history as he encountered it on his tours of the island.

Elli Beach

Further along the water's edge towards the northern tip lies **Elli Beach** with the once-fashionable Elli Nightclub and adjacent yachting marina where yachts can be hired from the clubhouse. There are some public tennis courts nearby and the once-famous luxury Hotel des Roses. Constructed in Moorish style by the Italians in 1926, it was the first holiday hotel to be built on the island, but it now stands empty and abandoned. Plans have been mooted to renovate the hotel and convert part of it into a casino, but as yet they have not been realised. The walk ends at the ★ **Aquarium** (daily 9am–4.30pm) ❹❽ where examples of nearly every kind of fish and sea creature in the Aegean can be seen.

Walk 6

Monte Smith – The Acropolis and Necropolis of Ancient Rhodes

Sunset from Monte Smith

To the southwest of the town lies the Acropolis hill. It was known as Mount Stephanos in Byzantine times but the Ottomans renamed it **Monte Smith** after the English admiral William Sidney Smith (1764–1840). During the Napoleonic Wars the English allied with the Turks against Napoleon and the admiral used the hill to observe the movements of the enemy fleet.

Opposite: the Temple of Apollo

View from Monte Smith

Swedish and Italian archaeologists have cleared away the rubble from the ancient ruins and in fact little remains of them. They do, however, still give a clear impression of how the acropolis once looked. Even those with little interest in sites of antiquity will find it worth the climb to the top of the hill for the magnificent view across to Asia Minor and for the peace and quiet. Watching the sun set from Monte Smith is a memorable experience. The bus from the Nea Agora takes only a few minutes, but if more time is available, then make the climb on foot. Foundation walls, water pipes, sections of cobbled road and other smaller excavated sites can be identified from the road and offer an insight into the sheer size of the ancient town. To walk to the top of the hill from the Amboise Gate will take about 20 minutes.

At the summit of the **Acropolis Hill** (111m/365ft) ❹❾ once stood the **Temple of Athena and Zeus**. It is impossible to imagine its beauty from the huge sections of broken columns and simple Doric capitals which are scattered around. The ★ **Temple of Apollo** can just be identified from the rather sparse foundations. Italian archaeologists reconstructed a corner of the temple, resting a fragment of the entablature above three whole Doric columns. A better impression can be gained of the **stadium**, which has been almost completely restored and the **amphitheatre**, complete with marble staircases, which has also been rebuilt. It was once able to accommodate 800 spectators and was probably used by the famous School of Oratory (*see page 67*) which was based in the **Rodini Valley** about half-an-hour's walk from the acropolis. It is perhaps difficult to imagine a college in which the students did not sit in closed lecture halls but conversed with their tutors in the open air. Clearly the shady valley was the perfect spot for this informal teaching style. The Greeks probably created a garden with statues and seating beneath the trees. This idyllic parkland beside a tiny stream sandwiched between the foot of Monte Smith and the road to Lindos stands as an oasis of peace at the edge of the busy town and is a popular destination for Rhodian families.

The amphitheatre

A local guide

In antiquity the Rodini Valley lay outside the town walls and became the burial ground for inhabitants of the old city. Many ancient graves have been discovered in the vicinity, including some rock tombs and the ★ **Tomb of Ptolemy**, as it is known. This 4th-century BC tomb carved out of the rock is unlikely to have been the last resting place of Alexander the Great's general but it was given the name by northern travellers in the 18th and 19th century. The locals call it *koufio vouno* or hollow mountain. Only the north facade of this 28-m (90-ft) square tomb remains relatively intact, but originally 21 plain half columns lined the four sides. The burial chambers are not open to visitors.

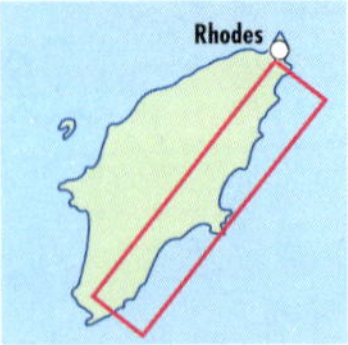

Route 2

The East Coast – beaches, monasteries and knights' castles

The appeal of the island's east coast lies in its sheltered beaches, ancient sites, old monasteries and churches with frescoes. The highlights, apart from Lindos, include the lonely forest of Epta Piges (Seven Springs) and the Oriental-style baths at Kalithea. Allow about 2 days to travel this route.

Travelling by bus

Buses: regular scheduled bus services run down the east coast from Rhodes City to the villages and back several times a day – half-hourly and hourly to the closer destinations. There are also interconnecting bus services between villages.

Ready for takeoff

The journey along the coast road from Rhodes City to Lindos lasts no time at all and it takes barely another hour to reach the south coast. It is possible to make a full tour of Rhodes in one day but to cover 220km (136 miles) in such a short time is to miss the full beauty of the island. Hotels are situated in isolated spots along the coast which becomes more rugged as the road progresses south and there ought to be no problem finding a bed in one of the southern villages such as Gennadi or Lahania. The beaches there are just as beautiful as those in Faliraki or Koskinou but much less crowded.

The tourist hotels and popular beaches at **Agia Marina** are not far from Rhodes City. **Koskinou** 9km (5½ miles) away lies a little way inland. During the Ottoman period it was one of only four villages inhabited by Turks and a Turkish minority still live here. It is worth making a brief halt in Koskinou as it is one of the prettiest villages on the island. A number of houses were built in the traditional style of the 17th and 18th century and a few which date from the turn of the century were constructed in a neo-Classical style. The colourful facades are particularly striking, as are the brightly painted doors and entrances which stand out against the otherwise plain chalk whitewash. **Agia Irini**, a domed basilica dating from the 13/14th century, is situated on the edge of the village. It is no longer used for services and the frescoes inside are in poor condition. A minor road leads down to the coast.

Kalithea Beach

The small beach at ★ **Kalithea** 10km (6 miles) from Rhodes City can get very crowded. Hippocrates, the father of modern medicine, advised his patients to take the water at Kalithea as it was thought to be beneficial for kidney and arthritic complaints and in antiquity the spa attracted visitors from as far away as Egypt and Syria.

However, the special healing powers were later forgotten about. During the 1920s the Italians sought to restore the **thermal baths** to some of their earlier splendour. They laid out a terraced tropical garden and built domed pavilions with pink marbled pillars, arcades and covered walks in a pseudo-Moorish style, but the hot mineral waters did not prove to be an enduring attraction and the grandiose, palm-shaded structure is now in a sorry state. The charm of Kalithea itself, however, is sufficient to attract visitors who keep coming well into October when the water in the deep, sheltered bay starts to cool.

Kalithea thermal baths

Faliraki 8km (5 miles) further on is the St Tropez of Rhodes. Huge hotels offer similar facilities and the choice of restaurants is vast. The wide flat beach extends for miles and is ideal for young children and non-swimmers. The southern end of the beach is marked by **Cape Ladiko** and the Anthony Quinn Beach, so called because after *The Guns of Navarone*, featuring the actor, was filmed here, the islanders made him a present of it. Faliraki has the only nudist beach on Rhodes.

Unlike Faliraki, **Afandou**'s miles-long beaches are shingle and there are no big hotels. The only golf course on Rhodes is situated here between the beach and coast road. The sleepy village of Afandou (pop. 1,500), whose main occupation is carpet weaving, lies in a dip about 2½km (1½ miles) from the beach (*afantos* means hidden or invisible). Studios and holiday flats can be rented here and there are a number of tavernas and cafés.

Further down the coast in **Kolymbia**, a long avenue of eucalyptus trees leads down to **Kolymbia Beach**, one of the prettiest on the east coast. There are plenty of good new hotels to choose from, but it is a much quieter resort than Faliraki.

Inlet at Cape Ladiko

Epta Piges

Tsambika Monastery

Castle at Arhangelos

★ **Epta Piges** or Seven Springs lies 4km (2½ miles) inland in fertile land – a cool, shaded spot, which according to legend was favoured by the nymphs. Here it is possible to sit for hours in a simple café in the woods, soothed by the waters of a babbling brook and cooled by the impenetrable shade of ancient plane trees. Peacocks strut proudly between the tables.

The small Seven Springs reservoir can be reached either through a 150-m (500-ft) long and 1.8-m (6-ft) high tunnel (a torch is recommended) or along a path over the hill. A number of rare orchids such as the violet-blue limodorum or the mysterious mandrake with its bright blue flowers and thick, yellow fruit can be seen in late summer. The mandrake root is said to resemble the human form and during the Middle Ages strange magical powers were attributed to it.

South of Kolymbia at the top of the 326-m (1,070-ft) ★ **Mount Tsambika** stands a simple monastery and place of pilgrimage dedicated to the Virgin Mary (*Panagia*). The winding road ends at a car park. The last section, a steep, concrete footpath, must be negotiated on foot (15 minutes). But the fine view from the summit will provide some compensation. On the return journey, the Panorama View Taverna in the car park will help to revive spirits.

According to legend, women wishing to conceive should spend the night in the monastery, where a simple chapel contains an 11th-century icon of the Virgin. Boys should then be called Tsambikos and girls Tsambika, both typical Rhodian names. Every year on 8 September, both here and in the new Tsambika monastery on the coastal road, special services are held and a pilgrimage made in honour of the *Panagia*.

Pottery is the main industry in ★ **Arhangelos** (pop. 5,000; 32km/20 miles from Rhodes City) and visitors are welcomed in the many factories. The wares are no cheaper than anywhere else, but the choice is wider. The local women also sell hand-made textiles.

The **castle** built by the Knights of St John Grand Master Jacques de Milly in 1457 offers a superb view of the unusual bell tower and the houses nestling among the orange groves. The castle was built as a defence against pirate attacks but only a few ruined walls remain. Large, well-maintained houses in the village testify to the prosperity of the inhabitants and many have colourfully painted walls or else the whitewash is broken up by sea-blue, pink or yellow doors and wall edging.

The church in Arhangelos, ★ **Agios Ioannis Prodromos**, boasts 14th- and 15th-century fresco fragments and another church the ★ **Agii Theodori**, barely 2km (1¼ miles) south along the coast road, has frescoes which are still in good condition.

The beach at **Stegna** lies some 3km (2 miles) away to the north of Profitis Ilias (not to be confused with the mountain of the same name in the west of the island) and is still a very quiet spot. There is a small fishing harbour, several cheap but none the less good tavernas and a number of pensions.

Close to a pretty, curved bay and at the foot of the huge, abandoned ★ **Feraklos** fortress – it was the first that the Knights of St John captured in 1306 – lies the old fishing village of **Haraki**. Several cafés and tavernas (the **Argo** fish restaurant enjoys a good reputation) line the promenade above the beach and accommodation is available in apartments, pensions and studios.

The coast road turns off to Lindos (*see pages 43–7*) a few miles beyond Kalathos beach at Vlicha Bay with its three A-category hotels (*see page 93*). **Lardos**, a favourite with British tourists, lies a little further south. Plenty of tourist hotels can be found by the beach, but there are a number of family-run establishments in the pretty village situated 2km (1¼ miles) inland.

★★ **Thari Monastery**, a Byzantine jewel, can be reached easily from Lardos. Head inland for about 12km (7 miles) to **Laerma**, a mountain village populated mainly by older people. The monastery, which was abandoned a few years ago, is in a clearing to the south at the end of a bumpy road. One monk lives on the premises and keeps the church open. Few visitors find their way here and those who do will have the spacious monastery to themselves and will be able to appreciate the uncanny tranquillity of this remote spot.

According to local legend, a Byzantine princess was cured of an otherwise incurable disease in the solitude of the woodland and she had the church built as a token of her gratitude. Dedicated to the Archangel Michael, the dome and walls are completely covered with well-preserved frescoes. Showing scenes from both the Old and New Testament, some date from the 14th century, but the majority were painted during the 16th and 17th centuries. Evidence of the influence of the Cretan school can be seen in the *Last Supper*.

Take the same route back to the east coast or continue south along the track from the car park to the coast via ★★ **Asklipio**. Although at first sight the road may not look passable, it is fine for cars. Here the ruins of the southernmost fortress on the island dominate the small mountain village. However, the real gem is the late Byzantine domed basilica known as ★★ **Kimisis Theotokou** (daily until 3pm). The date 1060 stands above the portal, but the true date of construction must have been several decades later with the two side aisles being added in the 18th century. Inside are paintings dating from 1646 and

Haraki fish taverna

Thari Monastery and priest

Kimisis Theotokou interior

Gennadi

A prize catch at Plimiri

1677, although some in the chancel and inside the dome were overpainted in 1923. There is a fine view of the little church and the surrounding green hills from the terrace of the **Agapitos** café. It is sad but inevitable that this village, whose inhabitants are mostly quite old, will probably be deserted in a few years time, as there is little to keep young people here.

Gennadi (64km/40 miles from Rhodes) has developed into a busy resort like Lardos, if perhaps a little quieter. Rooms are available in small family-run hotels in the village or by the beach about 1km (½ mile) away.

The beach at **Plimiri**, 12km (7 miles) south of Gennadi and 6km (4 miles) from Lahania, is often deserted. There are no hotels and only one taverna, but the romantic view over the little fishing bay makes it easy to linger. **Lahania** is like most of the villages in the south – depopulated. The young people have moved to the towns to find work and only return at holiday time. Their parents stay behind on their own. Even in Greece the traditional extended family is disintegrating. The only compensation is the arrival of young western Europeans who buy old properties and enjoy restoring them.

Surfing Taverna at Prasonisi

The southernmost village in Rhodes is **Kattavia** where strong prevailing winds and large breakers make windsurfing the main attraction. From Kattavia, a 9-km (6-mile) track leads due south to ★ **Prasonisi Beach**, where two small hotels and two tavernas (where fresh fish is a speciality) are the only tourist facilities. West and east coasts meet at the Prasonisi peninsula, which is actually a tiny island joined to the mainland by a sandbar. If this isn't flooded (as is often the case in winter), visitors can take the half-hour stroll to the lighthouse at the other side.

A successful outing

Route 3

★★★ Lindos – the prettiest village on Rhodes.

Snow-white houses beneath the huge acropolis, narrow winding lanes with pebble mosaics for pavements and two beautiful bays make Lindos the prettiest spot on the island of Rhodes.

View of the bay at Lindos

Buses: There are about 10 to 15 buses per day to Rhodes City. In summer, the non-stop Lindos Express links the two towns.

Lindos (pop. 1,600) lies 49km (31 miles) southeast of Rhodes City. Its inviting coastal landscape is a combination of gentle hills and abrupt slopes, and village houses stand in an arc nestling beneath the barren rock with views across the peninsula that divides the bay in two. The imposing medieval knights' buildings fringe the acropolis which soars high above the sea.

History

That Lindos emerged so early as such an important and prosperous maritime and commercial centre is due to its natural harbour which is now badly silted up. There used to be a saying '10 Rhodians – 10 ships', but it really referred to the Lindian seafarers, who built superb ships in their own shipyards.

Lindos did not trade just with the merchants of the Aegean ports, but with the Phoenicians, the Egyptians, and the inhabitants of the Balearic islands, and it also founded colonies in southern Italy and Sicily. Trade was made easier by the use of coinage and Rhodian maritime law, which was later adopted by Augustus for the Roman Empire and survived until Byzantine times. Lindos soon eclipsed the two other city states on Rhodes – Kamiros and Ialysos.

The city enjoyed its greatest prosperity under Kleoboulos, one of the Seven Sages, in the 6th century BC. During his 40-year reign, he built a stone temple to the goddess Athena Lindia which replaced the 7th-century BC wooden shrine situated above the ancient Lindian sacred grotto. At the end of the 5th century BC, the three city states combined forces for defence purposes and in 408BC created the city of Rhodes.

An enduring form of transport

As a result, Lindos lost its political importance but retained considerable commercial advantages. Its continuing wealth was reflected in the grand buildings constructed to replace the Athena Lindia Temple which burnt down in 392BC.

The decline of the city began during the Roman empire and the appeal of the shrine waned. Little is known of Lin-

Tablecloths for sale

dos' fortunes during the Byzantine period. A castle was built on the acropolis and the inhabitants sought shelter there when pirates attacked. The Knights of St John later built houses beneath the impressive fortress and began to create a new village above the ancient settlement, drawing on the town's old seafaring traditions.

The whole town is now protected by a preservation order and much of the ancient site will remain buried beneath the soil. The acropolis and its environs were, however, excavated by Danish archaeologists between 1909 and 1912 and the Italians later undertook extensive reconstruction work.

★★ *The Acropolis of Lindos*

The climb up to the acropolis is not too arduous, although a certain amount of care is required in negotiating the steps, which uncountable feet have worn smooth. Be sure to wear shoes with a good grip. Donkey taxis are another option. Lindian women sit at stalls en route to the citadel selling their tablecloths and embroidery.

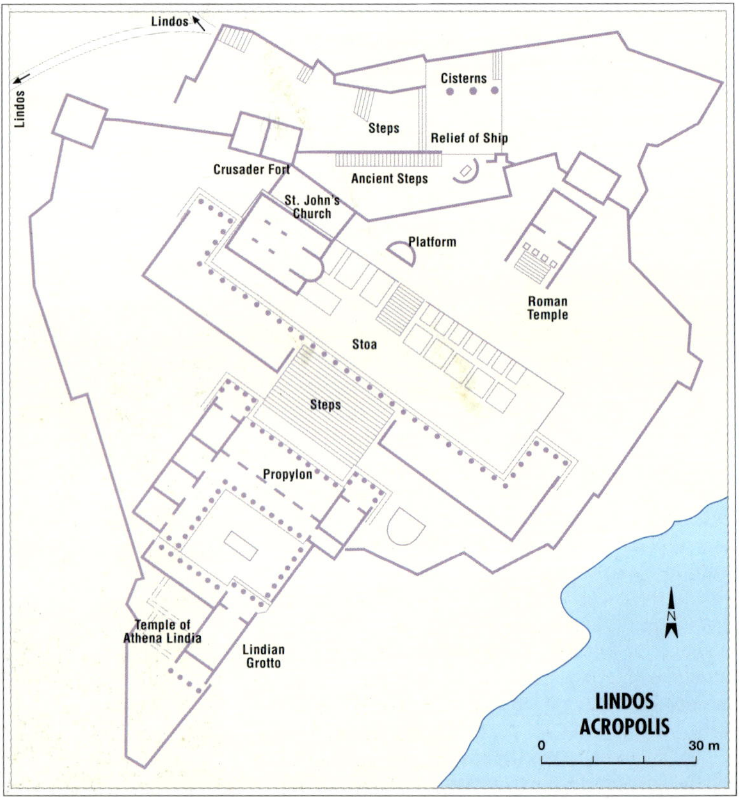

First of all stop at the ★★ **Exedra of Lindos**, a small platform with an unusual rock carving. It shows the almost life-size stern of a Hellenistic military vessel known as a *trireme* and demonstrates the high status of sea voyages. Dating from the beginning of the 2nd century, an inscription states that the carving was the work of the sculptor Pythocritus, who also created the *Nike of Samothrake* (now in the Louvre). It is thought the carving was endowed by the Lindian admiral Aghesandros.

Exedra of Lindos

A steep flight of steps leads from the ship relief up to the entrance of the Crusader fort. It was built either under the Grand Master Antoine de Fluvian (1421–37) or Grand Master Pierre d'Aubusson (1476–1503). Both coats of arms can be seen above a window in the Commander's house. The course of the ancient steps can be discerned to the left of the portal. The entrance to the acropolis would probably have stood roughly where it does now.

Among the ruins

A vaulted hall links the steps with the Fort Commander's rooms which are now used as a museum. The east side is all that remains of the 13th-century Byzantine St John's Church which leans against the upper storey. Further east on the first large terrace stands another exedra (3rd century BC) with a statue of Pamphilidas, a wealthy Athenian priest. The foundations of a small Roman temple are also visible here.

A flight of steps leads into the huge Doric **stoa**. Only 20 of the original columns are still standing. The architects had the clever idea of omitting the back wall behind the middle eight columns so that the view of the grand staircase leading up to the propylon would not be impeded and light could pass through. The **propylon**, of which only the foundations remain, dates from the 4th century BC and was modelled on the propylon at Athens.

The ★★ **Athena Lindia Temple** (Tuesday to Friday, 8am–5.40pm, Saturday and Sunday 8am–3pm) seems small and modest by comparison to the flight of steps and colonnade, measuring not quite 22m (72ft) in length and about 8m (25ft) wide with four columns on both short sides. The decision to build the temple on the southwestern tip of the hill and at the highest point of the steep-sided rocky plateau was made for two reasons: the sacred ancient Lindian grotto was situated just below and all sides could be seen from the sea. In 392BC the temple burnt down and out of respect for the hallowed site, the same plan was used for the replacement 50 years later.

The Athena Lindia Temple

The Lindian Temple Chronicle *(see page 66)* tells of the splendour of the shrine, the valuable sacred offerings made by mythical heros such as Minos, Hercules, Menelaos and Helen, as well as historical personalities such as Alexander the Great and Pyrrhus. The marble stele recounts three manifestations of the goddess Athene. One occurred at

The alternative to walking

a time when the Persian king Darius was attacking Greece. As his fleet under Datis, the commanding officer, reached the coast of Rhodes '...the surprised islanders gathered on the acropolis at Lindos where they endured the Persian siege until the water ran out. The goddess Athena appeared to one of the archons in a dream and told him that she had asked Zeus to send them water. The Lindians plucked up courage and told the Persians that they would surrender if Zeus did not send rain within five days. When Datis heard of this he laughed, but on the next day he saw a black cloud forming above the acropolis and the rain about to pour down in just that one spot. By this time the Persians had no water left either. Out of respect for the goddess, they made a valuable sacrifice'.

Built on the highest point of the acropolis, the Athena Lindia Temple offers a splendid view over the roofs of Lindos and the bays on either side of the peninsula. The circular bay seen to the south is called the **Bay of St Paul** as in AD51 the apostle Paul is said to have sought shelter there on his way to Palestine. Precisely 1900 years later, in 1951, the Agios Pavlos Chapel was built to commemorate his visit. The bay has two tiny beaches which are less crowded than the beach at Lindos itself.

The Bay of St Paul

A pleasant hour-long stroll along the northern bay will lead to the isolated ★ **Tomb of Kleoboulos**. Situated on a rocky outcrop in the bay and looking down over Lindos, it is just one of many tombs found near the village. This simple Hellenistic circular chamber is not thought to have contained the sage, but was probably the tomb of a wealthy Lindian family. In Christian times, it was converted into a chapel and dedicated to St Emilianos.

Another ancient site worth a visit is the 4th-century BC ★ **theatre** on the southwest slope of the acropolis, which used to accommodate about 2,000 spectators.

★★ The Village of Lindos

Lindos is now designated as a National Historic Landmark and there are no concrete buildings to be seen anywhere. The 'Captains' Houses' date from the 17th century when Lindos' seafaring traditions revived. The wealthy mariners used the Crusader architecture of Rhodes City as their model. Door and window surrounds, sometimes even complete walls, are exquisitely ornamented. The pointed Gothic arches show clear traces of Moorish influence and a cross reminiscent of the Order of St John was carved into the lintels.

In summer many of the courtyards with their black and white pebble mosaics *(kochlaki)* turn into main living rooms and provide an insight into Mediterranean home life. The first room off the courtyard is the *sala*, the family's reception and bedroom. Its walls are usually covered with the famous 16th- and 17th-century Lindian plates and decorated with embroidered fabrics. In one corner hangs the *sperberi*, a brightly coloured bed cover. Many of these delightful handicrafts can be seen in the Rhodes City Museum of Folk Art. Separated from the rest of the house and usually situated above the entrance facing the sea is the 'Captain's Room'. A few of the houses are open to visitors and many are let to tourists.

Towards the end of the 19th century, returning emigrants began to build large houses in neo-Classical style. Several of these buildings, which resemble ancient temples, can be seen throughout the town.

Mosaic courtyard

Souvenir plates

The ★★ **Panagia** (Church of the Assumption of our Lady) (daily, 9am–3pm) is said to have been built in the 14th century and then restored under the Grand Master Pierre d'Aubusson in 1490. The simple zigzag patterns of black and white pebbles on the floor of this domed basilica are particularly striking. Well-preserved frescoes telling the story of the Creation adorn the walls and an inscription attributes them to Gregory of Symi, around 1780.

The Akathystos hymn – a song of praise to the Blessed Virgin – is represented in 24 pictures, which begin in the south nave, follow the west wall and end in the north nave. The hymn is sung standing up, which is the meaning of *akathystos* and is only sung during Friday services in Passiontide, the four-week period of fasting before Easter.

Of the other tiny churches in Lindos, the subterranean ★ **Agios Georgios Chostos** deserves mention. It dates from the 8th or 9th century, making it the oldest Byzantine church on the island. It has non-iconic frescoes dating from the iconoclastic era when it was considered blasphemous to represent images of Christ and the saints. Look out for frescoes from other periods including the colourful 12th-century ★★ *Portrayal of Five Saints.*

Sorting nets at Kamiros Skala

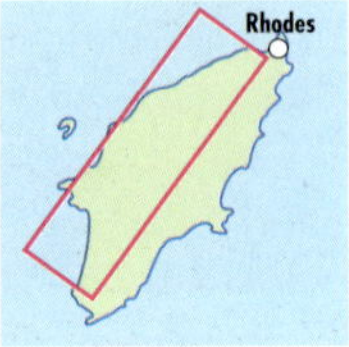

Route 4

The West Coast – mountains, cliffs and lonely islands.

Allow at least two days for this route which leads down the west coast past rugged cliffs and miles of beaches – accompanied by the *meltimi* which makes the climate considerably fresher here than on the east coast. No one could leave Rhodes without paying a visit to the famous Valley of the Butterflies at Petaloudes.

Buses: a regular bus service leaves Rhodes City several times daily – half-hourly and hourly for closer destinations – for most villages along the coast, with other services connecting villages inland.
Ferries: in the summer a ferry leaves Kamiros Skala every day for Khalki. The crossing takes 75 minutes.

The wild west coast

The long, fine shingle beaches immediately to the south of Rhodes City which extend past Kritika, Ixia and Ialysos (Trianda) are the package holiday playgrounds, but few who stay here will come into contact with Greek people and experience the Greek way of life.

Only south of Kamiros Skala does the windy west coast become wilder. Tall rocky ridges and steep foothills shaped into bizarre formations by the elements come into view. Every incline on the road affords new, dramatic views over the sea and the bare islands. Few speculators have ventured into the villages in the south, a part of the island where little has changed in recent decades. The visitor here is still regarded as the *xenos*, the guest, and not the *touristis*, a new word which would not have been found in any Greek dictionary 30 years ago.

The town of **Ialysos** 8km (5 miles) from Rhodes City used to be called **Trianda** (Thirty), as 30 of the Knights of St John had their summer villas here. It is now known by either name. A 5½-km (3-mile) road which winds up ★ **Mount Filerimos** to the remains of ancient **Ialysos** (*see page 55*) starts here. The international airport lies between Kremasti and Paradisi and at the height of the season the noise can be intrusive.

Nevertheless, **Kremasti** is a popular resort with countless bars, cafés, restaurants and tavernas geared towards the tourist industry. At the entrance to the town stands the modern Church of the Virgin Mary or **Panagia Kremasti** funded by emigré Greeks, most of whom now live in the USA. The interior is beautifully appointed and contains an icon with miraculous powers. According to local legend, the picture of the Virgin Mary was found hanging in an olive grove, hence the village's name (*kremasti* means hanging) and every year between the 14 and 23 August, the villagers celebrate the Assumption of the Virgin with nine days of church services, fetes, dancing and other events, making it one of the biggest festivals in the Dodecanese.

Some 3km (2 miles) further along, the road branches off to the ★★ **Valley of the Butterflies** (*see page 57*) one of the island's main attractions at **Petaloudes**. In fact it is moths that arouse so much interest. *Callimorpha quadripunctaria* are more commonly known as the Jersey tiger moth and each summer thousands of visitors come to witness the mass gathering of these beautiful creatures. The moths are nocturnal and if disturbed from their daytime sleep by a clap of the hands they will fly off in dense swarms revealing their brightly coloured red and black spots and white stripes on the underside of their wings. Unsuccessful attempts have been made to breed them elsewhere and it has only been discovered recently that they are attracted by the distinctive scent of the oriental amber *(liquidambar orientalis)*, itself a rare specimen only found in Greece.

However, the disruption to their routine caused by the visitors is sapping their strength and endangering their existence. Numbers have been declining for several years now, as peace and quiet are essential for their survival. But even without the moths, only visible in July and August, this extraordinary place is worth a visit.

A minor road crosses the island to the east coast resort of **Afandou** (*see page 39*) passing through **Psinthos** where a number of basic tavernas and cafés in the large square can be a source of welcome refreshments.

The holiday region ends beyond the pretty village of ★ **Theologos** (21km/13 miles south of Rhodes) about 1km (½ mile) from the coast. After that, head for the attrac-

Windsurfing off Trianda

Valley of the Butterflies

Endangered species

tive wooded region about 4km (2½ miles) from **Soroni** (25km/16 miles) quickly passing by the power stations and an oil storage depot. There at the **Agios Soulas** monastery pilgrims pay homage to St Soulas on 30 July every year after a grand festival with events such as donkey races on the day before. A little further down the coast lies **Cape Agios Minas** opposite the turning up to the ancient city of **Kamiros** (*see pages 52–4*). Visit the ruined site and then take a dip in the sea before enjoying a refreshing drink at one of the nearby tavernas.

Fishing boats at Kamiros Skala

Enjoy seafood in a local taverna

Kamiros Skala is the only fishing port on the west coast, so three tavernas can be relied on for freshly prepared seafood. The remains of an unfinished relief on a Hellenistic gravestone can be seen on a rock wall near the harbour and the village also has a ruined early Christian basilica. Both provide evidence that Kamiros Skala has been inhabited continuously since ancient times. Take the ferry from here to go to Khalki (*see page 63*).

Close to Kamiros Skala on a steep rock high above the sea lies **Kastellos**, a knights' castle which even as a ruin makes an impressive sight. Started in 1309, the tower and the walls were added in 1472. It must have played an important part in Mediterranean trade as it was financed by a Florentine bank.

Ruin of Kastellos

The main road continues into the snow-white village of **Kritinia** which, as the name reveals, was founded by Minoan Cretans. It has superb views over the beautiful coastal landscape and the deep blue sea so it is worth taking a look at Kritinia's main sight – **Agios Ioannis Prodromos**, a little church lying in the shadow of two tall cypresses at the southern end of the village. This tiny chapel was built in the 12th and 13th centuries and its frescoes, some of them badly faded, date from the 13th and 15th centuries.

Just before the mountain village of **Siana**, well-known for its honey and yoghurt, a minor road, perhaps a little treacherous at the end, leads down to the lonely beach at **Glyfada** 6km (4 miles) away. For anyone wishing to spend a little more time in this peaceful but bizarre landscape of woodland and rocky gorges, the **Mavroudis** pension makes a good base. In Glyfada Bay there is just one taverna and the landlord has rooms to let.

Kastrou Monolithos

In Siana the striking neo-Byzantine **Panteleimon Church** (1892), endowed by a rich emigrant, stands in stark contrast to the simple, old chapel opposite.

Another Crusader castle is to be found just over a kilometre (¾ mile) outside the village of **Monolithos** (which means one stone). This important refuge known as ★ **Kastrou Monolithos** perches on a huge 250-m (820-ft) high table rock and was built by the Grand Master Pierre d'Aubusson in around 1500. Only the walls are left, but enough of the structure remains to give a clear idea of the castle's proportions. From a distance this massive rock looks steep and inaccessible, but the steps can be climbed in a matter of minutes.

Apolakia at 86km (53 miles) from Rhodes is the southernmost village on the west coast and lies beyond a wide expanse of pine forest which has been devastated by fire, a scene which continues along the road to **Gennadi** 17km (10 miles) to the east and also the country roads leading to the villages of **Istrios** and **Profilia**. Apolakia (pop. 600) is a largish village and boasts several tavernas and cafés around the main square. Here Greek coffee is served in the traditional way with a glass of water – a practice that died out in the tourist citadels of the north many years ago.

Apolakia beach, which is some 10km (7 miles) long, is often totally deserted. Not far outside Apolakia towards Istrios and only accessible by a rough track is the simple late Byzantine ★ **Agios Georgios Vardas** chapel. This little gem displays rustic-style frescoes which date from its construction at the end of the 13th century. About 45 years ago, the early Christian church of Agia Irini was discovered there and, in 1993, road workers uncovered another 5th-century church near the village. An inscription states that the 30-m (100-ft) long building was dedicated to St Catherina. These discoveries and other finds suggest that this was a region of commercial and cultural importance in early Christian times.

Arnitha, an idyllic spot where more early Christian church ruins have been found, and **Messanagros** are both well off the beaten track. The simple **Kimisis Theotokou Church** in Messanagros dates from the 13th century. It was built on the foundations of two early Christian basilica and the walls incorporate masonry of ancient and early Christian origin.

To the west of the village about 4km (2½ miles) or an hour's walk away stands the ★ **Skiadi Monastery**. Dating from the 13th century, this place of pilgrimage in the mountains is steeped in legend. A small domed basilica, now the chancel, also dates from the 13th century and was incorporated into the new church of 1861. Pilgrims are drawn to the monastery, especially on 7 and 8 September, to pay their respects to the miracle-performing icon of the Virgin Mary. According to legend, the picture was painted by the gospel writer Luke. Every year at the beginning of Lent, the icon tours the surrounding villages after first crossing to the island of Khalki. On the Sunday before Easter, St Thomas' Day, it arrives in the church of **Agios Thomas** between Messanagros and Lahania where a grand festival takes place. The icon is then carried back to Skiadi.

To reach the east coast again or **Prasonisi** (*see page 42*) at the southern tip of the island carry on through **Katavia** (114km/70 miles).

Skiadi Monastery, inside and out

The ancient site of Kamiros

Route 5

★★ Kamiros – the city above the sea

The excavated ruins of this Dorian city lie amid a green and undulating landscape. Enjoy the views and absorb the history of this ancient settlement.

On the west coast of the island 34km (21 miles) from Rhodes City and 120m (393ft) above sea level lies Kamiros, the second and smallest of the three Dorian city states. This town, praised by Homer for its fine pottery and set between wooded hilly ridges, is an idyllic spot. Nevertheless, it is worth trying to get here early in the day as ancient Kamiros is on the tourist bus route. The view from the excavated site is perhaps not so spectacular as the view from Lindos, but this is compensated for by the green, undulating surroundings. The gently sloping terraces on which the town is laid out and the interwoven boxes which form the foundations of the dwellings make an unusual sight.

The view from Kamiros

History

Mythical tales and archaeological digs have provided evidence that Kamiros was inhabited in Minoan times. It is said that Althaimenes, grandson of the legendary king Minos of Knossos, was the founder and according to legend, Tlepolemos, a son of Hercules, lived here and led the heroes of Kamiros into the Trojan War.

With its strategically poor and unprotected location – at no time was the town surrounded by a wall – Kamiros never attained the importance of Ialysos or Lindos. It was a peaceful town for 'ordinary people' whose pottery was well known beyond the island as was the advanced work of the goldsmiths. Unfortunately there are few examples of the creativity of this era apart from the Fikelloura vessels which were found in the nearby necropolis and can now be seen in Rhodes City Archaeological Museum. Most finds were taken off to London, Paris, Berlin and Munich. Large parts of the site and necropolises have yet to be excavated so it is possible that other examples will eventually emerge.

Until recently, it was assumed that Kamiros had no harbour and that the pottery was shipped out of the island from Lindos – unlikely in a town dependent on exporting its

Parrot fashion

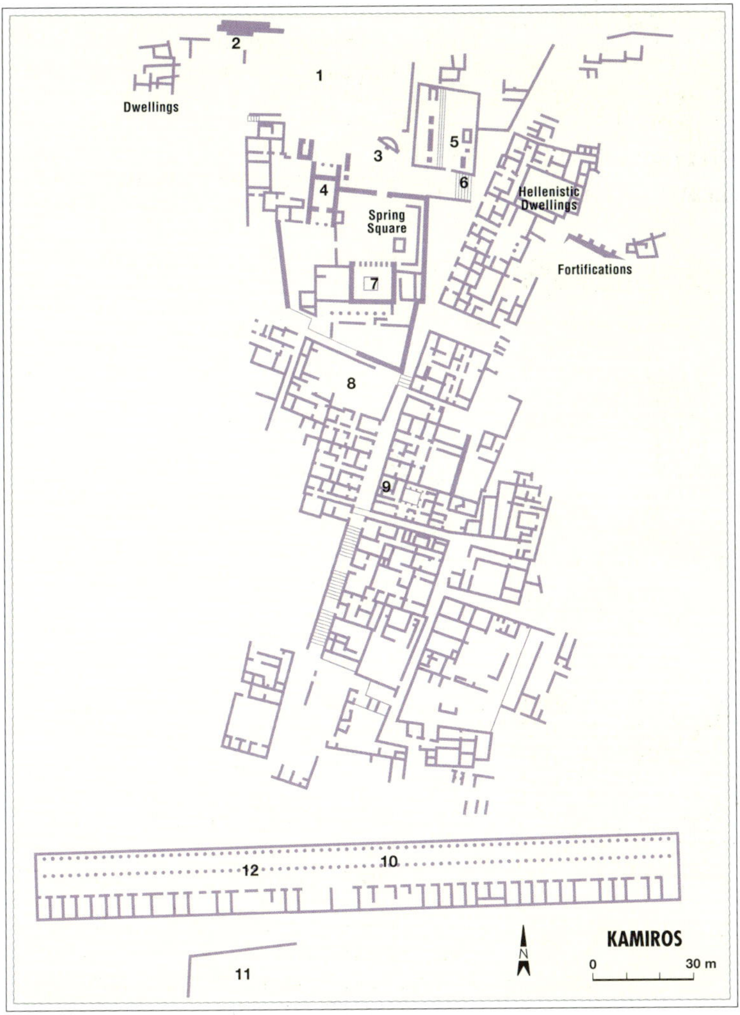

wares. The latest excavations by the coast road, on land south of the turning up to the ancient town, have unearthed proof that there must have been a port below the town.

After its destruction by an earthquake in 226BC, Kamiros was rebuilt in Hellenistic style, but another earthquake in AD142 finally persuaded the citizens to abandon the town and, unlike Lindos, it has never been resettled. The forgotten town was discovered by Salzmann and Biliotti in 1859. The site was carefully excavated by Italian archaeologists between 1929 and 1943 and is particularly interesting because the remains show a town inhabited by artisans who toiled in the many workshops and lived in the tiny houses, rather than by rich mariners and merchants. The temple district is modest compared to Lindos. The remaining fragments of the buildings provide clear evidence of Hellenistic planning, with its juxtaposition of natural and architectural features.

Ancient Kamiros

The steps from the temple

The Temple of Athena Kamira

A walk round Ancient Kamiros (Tuesday to Sunday, 8am–7pm, in winter 9am–3pm; *see map, page 53*). Start at the lowest terrace, the **Temple terrace [1]**, which is marked off by **supporting walls [2]**. Numerous column stumps with inscriptions and a sloping **exedra [3]**, a semicircular stone bench, suggest that statues and offerings to the Pythian Apollo once stood here. Only the substructure of the **Doric temple [4]** remains. A **square [5]** with two rows of altars extends on the east side of the Temple terrace. According to the inscription, the large altar to the right of the entrance was dedicated to the sun god Helios. The **flight of steps [6]**, which links the Temple terrace with the straight main road through the residential quarter of the town, would have served as a stand for spectators. On its way up to the acropolis, the main road passes a **well house [7]**, **baths [8]** and various largish Hellenistic dwellings often arranged around an atrium. At one of the finest atrium houses, the columns have been re-erected. This was the **villa [9]** of a prosperous citizen. In the alleys behind, the houses of the poor look somewhat less elegant.

Without doubt, the finest construction of this Hellenistic town was the **stoa [10]** which extended across the hilly ridge bordering the town in the east and overlooked the town and sea. In typical Hellenistic style, the 200-m (650-ft) long colonnade hid the **Temple of Athena Kamira [11]** – only a few fragments remain – so that its existence would surprise the observer as he emerged from the colonnade. The huge **cistern [12]** in front of the stoa was replaced by a fountain which then supplied the old town with water through a network of underground clay pipes.

Afterwards stop for a break in the shade of the vines at one of the tavernas by the sandy bay below or go for a swim in the sea.

Mount Filerimos: a panoramic view

Route 6

★ Ancient Ialysos on Mount Filerimos – a 'Friend of Solitude'

Known in antiquity as Achaea, the partly excavated ruins of this ancient Dorian town lie on a tranquil hilltop surrounded by dense pine forests.

Ancient **Ialysos**, the third Dorian town, lies on the 267-m (875-ft) **Mount Filerimos**, 10km (7 miles) south of Rhodes City. All that remains are the foundation walls of a 3rd-century BC Temple of Athena and a 4th-century BC Doric fountain. But the site has not been fully excavated and, judging by the size of the plateau, there is still plenty of the old settlement yet to explore. Evidence from the first settlement suggests that it dates from the Minoan/Mycenaean era. In antiquity, the town was called Achaea, but under the Dorians who settled on Rhodes in around 1000BC, it reverted to Ialysos, its earlier name and the one used in the myths and legends.

The town flourished in the 5th century BC but, after the amalgamation of the three Dorian towns in 408BC, it quickly lost its importance as the population emigrated to the new metropolis. The name Ialysos was soon forgotten as the town was abandoned.

In Byzantine times, hermit monks sought refuge on the hill and built a monastery directly on top of the ancient temple. The quiet, desolate hill was renamed Filerimos, or Friend of Solitude, by the monks. Although many tourists make their way here during the summer, it is still a fitting name for the tranquil rocky plateau.

Monastery icon

During the Italian occupation (1912–43), Italian archaeologists restored the Byzantine monastery, rebuilt some churches that the Crusaders had erected and re-

Forest on Filerimos

designed the grounds to create an attractive park shaded by cypress trees. It is surprising, however, that they undertook no systematic excavations and that the site was left freely accessible. (Tuesday to Friday 8am–6pm, Saturday to Sunday 8.30am–3pm).

The 5½-km (3½-mile) road which winds its way through dense pine forest to the top of Mount Filerimos offers fine views at every turn over the north of the island and the sea. Steps lead from the car park at the summit up to the **Church of Our Lady of Filerimos** which is now used for marriages and baptisms. It was built by d'Aubusson when he was Grand Master (1476–1505) and was then faithfully rebuilt in the Italian era. Restored monastery buildings surround the large inner courtyard, but the monks have long since departed. In front of d'Aubusson's chapel lie the remains of the 2nd/3rd-century BC **Temple of Athena and Zeus Polias**. The cruciform baptismal font near the d'Aubusson chapel is left from a triple-naved early Christian basilica, built in the 5th/6th century AD. Ancient masonry was used in its construction on a site directly above the southern section of the temple.

Monastery buildings

To the left, above the car park, a small chapel can be found built into the slopes. It is known as the **Agios Georgios Chostos** or the Burial Chapel of St George. The barrel-vaulted nave contains some well-preserved ★ **frescoes** which date from the Crusader era. The lower level of paintings on the side walls are the most interesting. They show how the Knights of St John were urged to join the order by their families' patron saints. The d'Aubusson coat of arms can be seen on the right-hand wall.

The Chapel of St George

A well-preserved ★ **Doric fountain** (300BC) stands on the southern slopes. It is of particular interest as such fountains are rare in Greece. The long basin is broken up vertically by pillars supporting a marble beam. The water used to spurt from lions' heads between the pillars and the inscription, part of which is visible on one of the pillars, gives instructions to users. In all, six Doric pillars adorned the front section.

Lines of cypress trees planted by the Italians lead from the car park to a ★ **viewing platform** which offers fine views over Rhodes City and the west coast of the island. The 14 copper icons on one side of the avenue represent the stations of the cross. Before leaving Filerimos, pay a visit to the kiosk in the car park which sells *Sette Erbe* (Seven Herbs), a herb liqueur originally made by monks. The drink is made in accordance with a recipe devised by Italian monks who lived here during the Italian occupation, which accounts for its Italian name, although it is sometimes known as *koleander*. You can also buy guidebooks, showing the layout of Filerimos.

Route 7

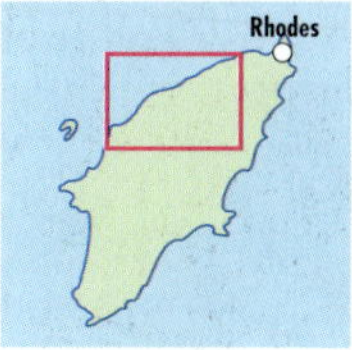

The Interior – pious pictures and mythical mountains

The green, wooded and mountainous interior is ideal for walking tours. The road passes through sleepy villages on the way to the summits of Ataviros or Profitis Ilias in the west, and jewels of Byzantine art are just waiting to be discovered. Allow two to three days for this journey.

Buses: several buses run daily from Rhodes City to Eleousa and back, and one bus a day to and from Embona, but there are no buses to the Profitis Ilias, so it is necessary to hire a car or take a taxi.

A local resident

There are two ways to reach the island's interior from Rhodes City. Either via the west coast as far as Soroni and then inland to Eleousa or the more pleasant route through wealthy **Maritsa** to **Psinthos** – the starting point for a detour to the **Valley of the Butterflies** (*see page 49*) – and on to the tiny village of **Archipoli** with its unusual bell tower. The road to Eleousa passes though mountain forests which are quite unlike others in western Europe: there are no proper paths to follow – most walkers will look in vain for the ones shown on the maps – and the way to the top is impeded by dense undergrowth and scree. Greek mountains are different. They are not just soulless geological formations, but important elements in Greek mythology. Gods were born and raised on their summits, saints were worshipped there and churches and monasteries constructed on their peaks.

In **Eleousa** enjoy an *ellinkos kafes* in the square that the Italians laid out, before visiting the simple 15th-century chapel ★ **Panagia Eleousa** on the edge of the village. Its naive wall paintings include interesting 17th- and 18th-century versions of the Creation and the Last Supper and although these frescoes do not have any special artistic merit, their powerful and imaginative style, no longer constrained by rigid iconography, leaves a lasting impression.

In a remote spot about 3km (2 miles) outside the village is the church of ★★ **Agios Nikolaos Fountoukli**, renowned for its frescoes and Byzantine architecture. Dedicated to St Nicholas, the patron saint of children, *fountoukli* means hazelnut. This chapel with its walls covered in frescoes was formerly part of a late Byzantine monastery, which has since disappeared. It was endowed by a top Byzantine official and his wife in memory of their three children who presumably died of the plague. Above the four-conch ground-plan (a square with four apses) towers a dome perched on a drum and broken up by narrow vertical niches and three brightly-painted Rhodian plates

Agios Nikolaos Fountoukli, interior details

Admiring the frescoes

are set into the wall over the portal. Some of the frescoes, which date from the 14th century, have been overpainted, others improved by the Italians.

In the slightly extended eastern conch – the chancel – stands an interesting portrayal of the Last Supper: on the left Peter accepts the bread from Christ and on the right Paul drinks the wine Christ has handed to him. The font is worth examining closely: one of the playful children is riding on a frog. Near the door on the west side, the benefactor can be seen offering a model of the church to Christ, while on the right are the three dead children, two boys and a girl, two of whose names can just be distinguished. One boy was called Georghios and the girl Maria. Vines with birds sitting on them indicate that the children are already in paradise.

The 14th-century cemetery chapel of ★ **Kimisis Theotokou** in **Salakos** is another of the three four-conch churches on Rhodes (the third is **Agios Georgios** in Rhodes City Old Town), which boasts a traditional Rhodian mosaic made from seashore pebbles. The fertile, wine-producing village, blessed with plentiful supplies of water, is the highest settlement on the island at 700m (2,330ft) above sea level and it will take about 1½ hours to walk there from Agios Nikolaos Fountoukli. In Salakos, there is one unpretentious guesthouse and a couple of tavernas around the shady square.

Convolvulus

A little-used road leads from the small Agios Nikolaos Fountoukli church up into one of the most densely forested areas on Rhodes and on to the island's third highest peak ★ **Profitis Ilias** (800m/2,625ft) which, with its rare botanical specimens, makes it a highlight of the island for nature lovers. A walk through the forests will reveal a wealth of Mediterranean flora. Many varieties of orchids thrive here as well as the violet Rhodian cy-

View from Profitis Ilias

clamen and the wild, white-flowering Rhodian peony. Two simple chalets just below the crest of the mountain, which look Tyrolean, form the **Elafos-Elafina hotel** which was built by the Italians. The name means stag and doe, a reference to the wild deer that roam the hillsides.

Practically every Greek island has a 'Profitis Ilias': it is usually the highest mountain, named after the Old Testament prophet Elijah (Greek *Ilias*) who ascended to heaven from a mountain top. There are in fact two mountains with this name on Rhodes. The other, which rises above the east coast near Arhangelos, reaches a height of only 500m (1,650ft).

★ **Ataviros** at 1,215m (3,985ft) is the highest mountain on the island and should really have been called Profitis Ilias. In antiquity, Mycenaean settlers recognised it as the tallest peak and built a shrine to Zeus, the father of the gods, at the summit. Only a few fragments remain today. The view from the top is magnificent with Crete visible on a clear day. The breathtaking panorama certainly makes the difficult climb worthwhile and in early spring it is a botanist's paradise – white and blue sage, bright blue anemones, cistus, red horned poppies and spurge carpet the wooded hillsides.

Start from Embona allowing 6½ hours for the return journey and, if possible, don't go alone. To enjoy the expedition to the full, take a room in the town and make an early start, perhaps even before sunrise, to avoid the hot midday sun at the steepest part. Take plenty of water and a packed lunch and wear strong walking shoes for protection against the thorny undergrowth.

Tourism has made quite an impact on the wine-producing village of ★ **Embona** 62km (38 miles) away from Rhodes City, but it is still a quiet spot. Many tour operators arrange what are known as 'Greek evenings' here as this is said to be one of the last villages practising the Rhodian way of life. Practically every house possesses a loom, and the women sell their embroidery, woven fabrics, small carpets and rugs in restrained colours and simple patterns at reasonable prices.

The Emery wine cellars are situated in Embona and the juice from the Athiri grapes which ripen on the western slopes of the Ataviros are bottled here (*see page 77*). To taste these high-quality wines, sampling sessions are held each weekday between 9am and 3pm. However, the wine can equally well be sampled in one of Embona's tavernas and the atmosphere in autumn when the plump grapes hang down from the verandas is worth savouring.

A mountain road leads down to the west coast. Kritinia is 7km (4 miles) away and Kamiros Skala (*see page 48*) is only another 3km (2 miles). A good way to round off the day is with a fish supper in one of the harbour tavernas.

Typical Hellenic colours

A choice of styles in Embona

Local wine and honey

Two trips to neighbouring islands

Opposite: Symi Island

★★ Symi

Enjoy the intriguing images of a bleak, rocky landscape and the pastel-washed facades of villas in the port of Yialos on Symi. One of the island's highlights is the picturesque Panormitis monastery.

Ferries: daily return crossings operate from Mandraki Harbour in Rhodes City to Symi.
Buses: on Symi a regular bus service runs between Yialos harbour and Pedi, and a special service links Yialos with the Panormitis Monastery.

The ferry crossing

Symi (58sq km/22sq miles) lies just off the Turkish coast about 24km (15 miles) from Rhodes. Do not miss the opportunity to visit this picturesque island. The view that meets the eye as the boat rounds the rocky coastline into the fjord-like harbour is stunning. Grand villas washed with pastel shades, some with neo-Classical facades, are stacked one above the other around the port of Yialos in the island's 19th-century main town, also called Symi. There are no modern hotel complexes here as Yialos is subject to a preservation order – the harbour, unusual clock tower (1881) and the administration building were used as a backdrop for the film *The Lost Island* starring Ben Kingsley.

As always, the island's origins are explained by a legend. Glaucus, a minor god of the sea and builder of Jason's Argo, is said to have carried off the Rhodian princess Symi to the island and later named it after her. Perhaps it was also Glaucus who taught the Symians shipbuilding as they prospered by building boats for the Knights of St John and the Turks. The latter showed their appreciation by rewarding the Symians with land on the nearby Turkish mainland along with a number of other privileges. Down the centuries, the island's extensive commercial links ensured prosperity and the sponge trade also provided a good source of income.

At the turn of the century, the island's population was in excess of 20,000, but many people subsequently emigrated and over the years numbers dwindled to about 2,500. Today, nearly all the islanders are involved in some way in the tourist industry and welcome the daytrippers from Rhodes, and as a result, the population has started to increase slowly with the return of many Symians from overseas – mainly from Australia. Tourism has provided the money to pay for the restoration of many of the fine old houses, and the larger captains' houses have been converted into hotels, obviating the need for modern concrete hotel blocks.

Sponges for sale

★★ **Symi** (pop. 2,500), the island's main town, consists of the harbour **Yialos** (bank, beach) and **Chorio** (village). The busiest time by the harbour is between 11am and 3pm when the cruise ships are moored alongside. Later, the town reverts to its usual leisurely pace. As few of the trippers choose to take the walk up the 500 wide steps of **Kali Strata** (Pretty Street) to the upper town of Chorio under the full glare of the midday sun, its narrow alleys remain quiet during the day. This climb is worthwhile, as it provides an excellent opportunity to study the condition of the houses which are not the victims of natural decay but were bombed by the German Luftwaffe during World War II.

The climb is worthwhile

Signposts point the way to Symi's small museum, which includes displays of ancient sculptures and Byzantine icons as well as folk art and curios from distant lands – souvenirs that the Symian seafarers brought back from their voyages. Only a few walls and arches remain from the medieval *kastro* on the ancient acropolis. For those with energy to spare, there is a rewarding view from the top of the fortress over the sea and also to the nearby Turkish island of Knidos. A number of windmills, some of which have been converted into attractive holiday flats, can be seen nearby.

Two other small settlements, **Nimborio** and **Pedi,** both have modest shingle beaches and can be reached easily by foot from Yialos in about 45 minutes. **Nanou Bay** is by far the prettiest of the other beaches and can be reached by motor boat. A number of tiny churches and monasteries, such as **Agios Fanourios** and the **Roukouniotis** monastery with its architecturally unusual chapel and 14th-century frescoes, are tucked away on the hillsides. A walk there from Yialos would take about two hours.

The main excursion from Yialos, however, is the 20-km (12-mile) journey to **Panormitis Monastery**, situated at the water's edge in the far south of the island. The monastery can be reached either directly by boat from Rhodes or by coach from Yialos. Dedicated to the Archangel Michael, it was founded in the 6th century, but its present appearance dates from the 18th century with the addition of the bell tower in 1905. Pilgrims visit the monastery church because of its miracle-performing icon of St Michael.

A veteran of the times

The inner courtyard – like the inner courtyard in the 18th-century church in Chorio (usually closed) – displays the distinctive pebble pattern typical of the Dodecanese Islands. The small museum in the monastery contains an impressive collection of old manuscripts, as well as icons and liturgical vessels. Tourists can stay overnight in the guest rooms at Panormitis.

Khalki

Enjoy a day or two on this remote island paradise, still untouched by the car and tourism.

Ferries: a 2-hour crossing daily from Kamiros Skala.

Khalki (28sq km/10sq miles), a bare, dry block of stone rising to 600m (1,950ft), lies only a few miles west of Rhodes and is probably more Greek than any other island in the Aegean. It is largely untouched by tourism and there are no cars or roads.

At the turn of the century, over 5,000 people lived on the island, but now there are barely 350 and they depend on fishing and visitors for their livelihood. However, although excursions from Rhodes have made a contribution towards raising otherwise very low incomes, it has not been enough to promote tourist facilities, and it can be difficult to find a room in high season as there are only a few privately run pensions.

During the last century, sponge divers became very rich, putting their lives at risk by staying underwater for hours on end with inadequate equipment. Khalki, Symi and Kalimnos derived considerable prosperity from sponge diving and some of the grand villas on these islands testify to the money which the activity yielded. The sponges the divers retrieved from the seabed were sought-after commodities in the bathrooms of the rich in Paris and other western capitals. The sponge itself, a mixture of plant and animal, looks far from appetising when it emerges from the sea. It is only after a long process of beating, drying and bleaching that it can be offered for sale. This precious material is now rare in Greece, as a fungal bacteria has wiped most of it out. Consequently, the sponges on sale on the islands now mostly originate from Sicily or North Africa.

In the town of **Nimborio** (sometimes referred to as Khalki) the imposing pastel-washed houses with their red roofs rise up the hillside in tiers. Many are empty, although a few have been faithfully restored with EU money. Village life is played out on the promenade where the Post Office, OTE and a few tavernas and cafés are.

The bathing beach at Pondamos Bay is a 15-minute walk away and in the summer, boats sail out to the uninhabited island of **Alimnia**, which has a fine beach and even finer bay. The road which leads past Pondamos Bay carries on into the deserted mountain village of **Chorio** (5km/3 miles) and a ruined Crusader fortress there offers splendid views. The intrepid traveller may wish to make the 3-hour trek from Chorio over bare limestone ridges to the lonely monastery of **Agios Ioannis**, where it is possible to spend the night.

Sisters at the helm

Sponge divers' boat

ΡΙΧΝΕΤΑΙ
ΤΟΝ ΟΒΟΛΟΝ ΣΑΣ

Art History

Salzmann and Biliotti were the first archaeologists to excavate on Rhodes and at the beginning of the 20th century Danish and Italian teams continued the task. Despite some long-established data, knowledge about the various eras remains fragmentary as most works of art were lost, having been taken to Rome in ancient times and later distributed throughout the museums of Europe.

Opposite: Agios Nikolaos Fountoukli

The ruins of Ialysos

Rhodian pottery

Apart from a few bronzes and some superb gold pieces, it is mainly pottery such as vases, craters, jugs and plates that remain from the Minoan and Mycenaean times (2nd millenium BC). The necropolises at Ialysos, Kamiros and Lindos were the main sources for these finds. Mycenaean pottery can be distinguished by its simple decorations of vertical bands, which skilfully emphasise the shape of the vessel, or stylised underwater flora like the octopus decorations which were popular on Crete.

Following the demise of the Mycenaean culture came the 'dark centuries' with Rhodes' artistic flowering emerging in the 'geometric period' between 900 and 700BC. Ornaments previously painted with sweeping brushstrokes were now decorated with mathematical patterns. Simple shapes such as circles, triangles, meanders, dots and lines were reproduced on pottery in many new variations using a compass or comb-like brushes. A number of craters from around 800BC with palm-tree and meander decorations are on display in the Archaeological Museum in Rhodes City.

In the 7th century BC, trade between Rhodes and Asia Minor and Egypt increased and this was also reflected in the vases. A completely independent pseudo-Oriental style developed which manifested itself in three different ways: the Euphorbos, Kamiros and Vlatos groups. Typical decorations were animal friezes – ibex and deer were very popular. Others showed drawings of strange creatures combining the features of more than one animal, mythical beasts and, more rarely, human figures interwoven with palmettes, lotus blossom and other floral designs.

Vase with human figures

A further development of the Kamiros and Vlatos group was the Fikelloura style – after the site near Kamiros where they were found – which dates from the 6th century BC. One of the finest examples is a water container with a partridge frieze (c 550BC) on display in the Archaeological Museum. Lotus blossom and buds grow up from the bottom of the vessel with two friezes painted with opposing half-moon-shaped lines above. At the top of the container are two stylised partridges which were said in antiquity to be able to ward off the evil eye.

Greek hero

A new city emerges

At the end of the 5th century BC, the three Rhodian city states of Lindos, Kamiros and Ialysos combined forces to create a modern town at the northern tip of the island, in the hope that together they could withstand the challenge of a powerful Athens. The model for the new town was the chequer-board layout at Piraeus, which the famous architect Hippodamos of Miletus had devised.

With its large and safe harbour, Rhodes City soon grew into a flourishing trading centre and its prosperous citizens built many new buildings, including a Temple of Helios. The site chosen for the shrine to the sun god is thought to be occupied now by the imposing Palace of the Grand Masters. Probably, statues of gods and Greek heroes would have adorned the temple and the surrounding gardens.

Rhodian sculpture from the Classical era (500–330BC) was used mainly for religious purposes and for honouring the dead. One of the finest examples of the sculptor's art is the funerary stele of Krito and Timarista (c 420BC) which was found in the necropolis at Kamiros (*see pages 52–4*) and is now exhibited in the Archaeological Museum in Rhodes City.

Rhodes Harbour

Rhodes flourishes

With its vast new harbour, Rhodes was able to maintain its status as a free state during the Hellenistic era (330–50BC). Art and science benefited from Rhodes' wealth. Both flourished and the city became, together with Alexandria, the cultural and scientific centre of the world. The Lindos Temple Chronicle is a marble slab (2.37m by 0.85m/7ft 9in by 2ft 9in) with inscriptions recounting the most important historical events of the Hellenistic period. It also contains valuable information about the Athena-Lindia cult.

A fine specimen

The school of sculpture

In the 4th and 3rd centuryBC sculptures became cherished objects, rather than just revered idols, and a commercial market emerged. A famous school of sculpture was established on Rhodes, attracting artists from all over Greece. Some of the illustrious scholars were Rhodians, the best known being Chares of Lindos. In the 3rd century BC he created the Helios statue, otherwise known as the Colossus of Rhodes. The Nike of Samothrake (190BC), now on display in the Louvre in Paris, is almost certainly the work of the Rhodian artist, Pythocritus.

Two other world-famous works which are no longer on the island are the Farnese Bull (Museo Nazionale in Naples) and the moving Laocoön group (Vatican Museum), a copy of which is on display in the Palace of the Grand Masters in Rhodes City. It shows the Trojan priest

Laocoön and his two sons in their death throes as they are strangled by snakes. Its discovery in 1506 on the Esquiline hill in Rome was witnessed by Michelangelo, and the single block of marble was immediately identified as the work of the Rhodian sculptors Athenodorus, Agesandrus and Polydorus. Renaissance artists celebrated the work as the most perfect of all time.

Two more superb late Hellenistic works are on view in the Rhodes City Archaeological Museum: a marble head of Helios (c 150BC)*(see page 23)* and the much-admired *Kneeling Aphrodite* (c 100BC)*(see page 22)*.

Paintings

Protogenes (c 330–300BC) was the most famous Rhodian painter but none of his paintings have survived. It is said that he painted extremely carefully and realistically, sometimes taking years to complete a picture. One of his paintings showed a resting satyr with a partridge sitting on a column and people claimed that the picture was so lifelike that the birds sang and twittered nearby as if it were a living creature. But Protogenes painted over the partridge as he felt that the bird eclipsed the satyr, which was his main figure.

The Rhodes School of Oratory

Around 330BC, the famous orator and politician Aeschines (389–314BC), a rival of Demosthenes (384–322BC) regarded by many as the greatest orator of all time, founded the Rhodes School of Oratory. It survived until 51BC and is said to have been located in the Rodini Valley. The spoken word was given greater weight in antiquity than it is today. For politicians and scholars, effective use of language was the best way to gain credibility, to enforce decisions and to maintain power. Attempts were made to approach the subject scientifically and textbooks on oratory were produced, some dating from the 5th century BC. Aristoteles wrote a three-volumed work on the subject.

The Greek education system, including the teaching of rhetoric, was adopted by the Romans in the 2nd century BC. As closer political links were forged between Rome and Rhodes in the 1st century BC, many Romans sought to arm themselves with the powers of persuasion that the School of Oratory provided. Almost every Roman of any importance studied in Rhodes at some time, including Brutus, Caesar's murderer, Cassius, Marcus Aurelius and Cato. Cicero, Caesar and Pompey attended on more than one occasion. The polymath Posidonius (131–51BC) taught at the school for several decades and wrote on an enormous range of subjects, including philosophy, history, astronomy and geography but only fragments of his writings survive.

Marble marvel

The face of an orator

The Temple of Apollo

Lindos: The Crusaders' fort and stoa

Architecture

The newly founded city of the 5th century BC extended further than the modern city and old town combined. Many public and sacred buildings were built including a stadium, odeon, the Temple of Aphrodite and the Temple of Apollo on Acropolis Hill. Many new buildings were also constructed in the other three Dorian cities. The Temple of the Athena Lindia, a propylon and a Doric stoa with a flight of steps were built in Lindos, a Temple of Athena on the acropolis in Kamiros and a Doric fountain and Temple of Athena in Ialysos.

Hellenism adopted the perfect harmony of Classical architecture, but the style was less austere and could be adapted to complement the background. A good example of the skilful 'stagecraft' of Hellenistic architects is the acropolis in Lindos. At the highest point on the rock the Athena Lindia Temple was built, hidden by a colonnade in front. Looking back through the columns of the stoa, another vista opened up over a magnificent landscape, invariably bathed in bright sunlight (*see page 45*).

Art treasures stolen in the name of Rome

After Rhodes became a Roman province (50BC–AD395), the economy of the island began to decline with serious consequences for its art. Few buildings of any note were constructed, apart from the Temple of the Emperor in Lindos. Out of more than 3,000 statues that had once stood in Rhodes City, the best were removed and in 42BC Cassius, who had once studied at the Rhodes School of Oratory, ordered most of the works to be taken to Rome. Many are now lost, although a copy of the Farnese Bull and the Laocoön group (*see page 67*) were discovered later.

Byzantine churches

In the 5th and 6th century, Rhodes enjoyed a new period of prosperity. Trade in the island's silk goods and agriculture flourished. So that Christianity, the newly adopted national religion of the Byzantine Empire, could be practised many new basilicas were built and decorated internally with paintings.

The oldest Byzantine church on Rhodes is the Agios Georgios Chostos in Lindos (*see page 47*) which has a domed hall, a design rarely seen in Greece. It consists of just one room and is decorated with frescoes dating from the time of the iconoclasts (8th and 9th century). Most of the decorations such as crosses and floral patterns are ornamental, but there are also pictures of ships and fishes which reflect Lindian maritime traditions.

Icons

Icons: the art of eternity

The interiors of very many Greek Orthodox churches are decorated with icons and frescoes. To many westerners the rigid and formal execution seems odd but, to understand about icons in the eastern Church, it is necessary to examine their function. Unlike western sacred art which aims to represent biblical scenes in a realistic way, Greek Orthodox art seeks to create a supernatural, mythical dimension in which the past, present and divine somehow merge with one another, so that the stories recounted in the Bible cease to be unique events and acquire an everlasting character.

By idealising concepts of the eternal and the sublime, the saint on the icon becomes ever-present. Just how difficult it is to express spiritual concepts using worldly forms was demonstrated by the response of the iconoclasts, the Greek Orthodox fundamentalists who set out to destroy icons and religious images (AD726–843). These opponents of icons saw it as blasphemy to portray Christ and the apostles figuratively, but the icon painters solved the problem by establishing a set of commonly understood formulae and symbols which allowed little room for individual expression.

The Knights of St John

The Knights' symbol

The Knights of St John held sway in Rhodes from 1309 to 1522. Their first undertaking was to build almost impregnable fortresses at strategically important places on the island to defend themselves from Turks and pirates who at that time were making the eastern Aegean region unsafe. The existing Byzantine fortifications at Lindos and at Rhodes City were extended and remain largely intact today. The local architects brought together the late Gothic style of the knights and the centuries-old traditional architecture of the island, thereby creating a charming mix-

Turkish gravestone

Entrance to the Turkish Library

ture of Byzantine-Aegean and late Gothic styles. This combination can also be seen in the Street of the Knights (Ippoton), where the houses are built very close together. It is the only completely preserved medieval residential street in Europe (for the Knights of St John, *see page 11*).

The Turkish era

The arrival of the Turks changed the character of the island's capital quite dramatically. The Ottomans extended the living quarters of the knights and converted all Byzantine churches into mosques. Some new buildings were constructed including the Turkish Library, and domed baths (both 18th century) which are still in use. Of the mosques that the Turks built, the most important is the Rejeb Pasha Mosque (1588) and the Mosque of Suleyman (1523–42). It has a simple square ground-plan and a plain interior. Typically Islamic stucco stalagmite-like features can be seen only on the dome. The minaret has been demolished as it was on the point of collapsing.

The 20th century

The Italians who occupied the island from 1912–43 completed several valuable projects such as new roads. Facilities for visitors including the Oriental-style thermal baths at Kalithea were built and historic buildings were renovated. They were also responsible for carrying out systematic excavations at the ancient sites. Using old engravings they set about rebuilding the Old Town of Rhodes City. Unfortunately, at least with the Palace of the Grand Masters, they failed to follow the original outline and there are doubts about its authenticity. In the new town, many new public buildings were erected, combining a series of architectural styles that included Moorish, Gothic and Venetian.

The Mosque of Suleyman

Rhodes and the Greek Myths

In his Seventh Olympian Ode, Pindar recounts how Zeus called together the gods to discuss how they would divide up the ancient world, but he forgot about Helios who had gone off in his sun chariot. When the sun god returned, Zeus was so upset at his mistake that he suggested reopening the discussion. But Helios had just seen an especially pretty island emerge from the sea, and asked if he could have it as a present, and Zeus agreed. Helios married the nymph Rhoda, the daughter of Poseidon. Their three grandsons were the founders of the Dorian cities of Lindos, Ialysos and Kamiros.

Other writers declared that the original inhabitants of Rhodes were the *telchines*, mysterious sea demons who were said to be the first to trade by boat with distant countries. They had lived on the island before it sank under the sea and, according to legend, had brought up the young Poseidon. He later married Halia, a sister of the *telchines*, who bore him six sons and one daughter, Rhoda, who then married Helios. Thus this account ties up with the first legend. The *telchines* were later associated with the 'evil eye' and came to represent the embodiment of evil.

Elsewhere in the Seventh Ode, Pindar reports that in Lindos, on the instructions of Helios, the Rhodians built the first shrine to Athene, daughter of Zeus. They forgot the fire, but neither Zeus or Athene were angry, as in the grotto beneath the acropolis the Lindians had revered an earlier deity, Lindia, by offering sacrifices without the use of fire. Lindia and Athene later became one and the same.

Another myth refers to the link with Crete. It was prophesied that Katreus, son of the Cretan king, Minos, would be struck dead by his son Althaimenes. So that he would not kill his father, Althaimenes sought exile in Rhodes and settled in Kritinia. On the summit of Ataviros, from where it was possible to see Crete on a clear day, he built a Temple of Zeus. Years later, Katreus expressed a wish to see his son, but when he landed at Kamiros, his son killed him, mistaking him for a pirate. In desperation, Althaimenes asked the earth to swallow him up, which it did.

The meaning of the word Rhodes is still something of a mystery. Many believe it goes back to the nymph Rhoda, who married Helios. Others trace the name to the flower on the coins – now on display in the island's Archaeological Museum, but the flower is not a rose, but a hibiscus. The name could also derive from the Phoenician word *rod* meaning snake, creatures which plagued the island until the oracle at Delphi advised that they could be eliminated by introducing deer. A bronze stag and doe still stand guard over the entrance to Mandraki Harbour, but Rhodes will always be the 'Rose Island'.

Helios' island

Temple of Athena Lindia

Displays of national dance

Festivals and Folklore

Easter in Greece

Easter is the main celebration for Greeks. It is a family festival and all flights, trains and buses will be fully booked as everyone tries to return home from wherever they are in the world.

Some of the traditions surrounding the Easter celebrations include fasting for 40 days beforehand, decorating churches with palm and laurel leaves, and stroking the bodies of pregnant women with a palm leaf. Good Friday is the day for ornate Easter processions with a flower-laden coffin of Christ carried through the streets. On Saturday, congregations gather for midnight mass and afterwards fireworks and candles accompany the worshippers home. Sunday is the day for a festive meal – usually barbecued lamb – followed by dancing and singing. The Greek Easter rarely falls at the same time as Easter in Roman Catholic and Protestant countries and sometimes it can be up to four weeks later.

Greek Orthodox Easter for 1996: 14 April; for 1997 27 April.

Summer Festivals

Enjoying a festival

Festivals are as much a part of Greek life as eating and drinking. They are a natural expression of fellowship and help to unite the community. Every village has at least one festival a year, usually to commemorate the saint to whom the village church is dedicated *(panagiri)*. Celebrations often begin on the day or evening before with music, dancing and plenty of food. On the saint's day, a service will be held and occasionally a procession will wind its way through the village.

Festival calendar

January: **1**. New Year's Day
6. Epiphanias. The Blessing of the Waters is held by the harbour.

March: Rose Monday (Kathara Deftera), takes place 40 days before Easter with processions in Afandou, Archangelos, Kremasti and Ialysos (Trianda).
25. Greek National Anniversary. The beginning of the War of Independence against the Turks on 25 March 1821 is celebrated with parades and wreath laying.

April: **23**. Feast of Agios Georgios (St George) in Kritinia.
Greek Orthodox Easter festival celebrated throughout the island at about this date (*see page 72*).

May: **1**. Labour Day.
First week in May. Flower festival celebrated in Rhodes City.
21. Feast of the Archangel Michael in Thari Monastery.

June: **29**. Feast of Agii Petros ka Pavlos (St Peter and St Paul) in Lindos.

July: **20**. Feast of the Prophet Elijah on Mount Profitis Ilias.
27. Feast of Agios Panteleimonas in Siana.
30. Feast of Agios Soulas in Soroni. Donkey racing, dancing and feasting take place on the previous day.

August: **6**. Metamorphosis or transfiguration of Christ at Maritsa.
15. Panagia Festival at Kremasti and Embona. The Kremasti festival lasts from 14 to 23 August and is a major celebration with traditional music and costumes.

September: **8**. Festival of the Virgin Mary in the monasteries at Skiadi and Tsambika.
14. Feast of the Holy Cross (Timios Stavros) in Apollona, Malona and Kalithies.

October: **18**. Feast of Agios Loukas (St Luke) in celebrated Afandou.
28. Ochi day. In 1940 the Greek dictator Metaxa rejected an ultimatum from Mussolini that would have allowed the Italian leader to station Italian troops in Greece.

December: **25/26**. Christmas
31. On New Year's Eve children receive presents from the Greek Santa Claus, St Vassilis. *Vassilopita*, cakes with lucky coins inside, are eaten.

Rhodes is made for flower festivals

Ready for the big race

ΚΑΝΘΑΡΟΣ
1992
PATRAS

Food and Drink

Opposite: Fish are usually grilled

The Greeks have contributed so much to European cultural history but have not yet discovered how to cook. Such a prejudiced view is often heard but is in fact far from accurate. The essence of Greek cuisine is simple recipes made from fresh ingredients. Plain, unadulterated Greek food is superb. What often disappoints, however, are the attempts by Greek restaurants to imitate western European dishes and this applies not just to the large hotels which have to cater for holidaymakers from all over Europe, but also to the better quality restaurants which offer so-called international cuisine.

Gourmets are also often heard criticising the lack of sequence to a menu. Greeks just do not organise their meals in this way. The dishes are ordered and then all served at the same time: salads, warm and cold starters, main courses, bowls and small plates with a range of delicacies are piled on to the table until there is no room left.

Eating out

When eating out, no Greek relies simply on the menu. He will do as he does at home and go into the kitchen to see what is cooking and perhaps base his choice on the appetising aromas.

For the Greek, eating is not just about filling an empty stomach but about fellowship. The conversation is just as important as what is on the plate. Families get together, invite friends and certainly do not exclude the children, right down to the baby. People who eat and drink alone in Greece are to be pitied. Little has changed since AD192 when the writer Athenaios wrote in his collection of essays *Banquet of the Learned*: 'If you see a man eating by himself, without company, you must recognise that he is losing half of his life and leads a wretched existence.'

A sociable event

Food and eating enjoyed high status in antiquity. Many famous chefs, including Agis of Rhodes, were not just cooks but also philosophers. Feasts in which the guests sat in a large circle would have been unthinkable without intellectual conversation and discussion.

Fresh from the sea

Starters: Greek cooking is best known for its *mezedes* or starters. The choice is so wide that a selection of *mezedes* could easily make a complete meal. For *mezedes*, a good restaurant will offer *taramosalata* (smoked cod roes blended with bread and olive oil), *melitsanosalata* (aubergine salad), *tsatsiki* (yoghurt with fresh cucumber, a little lemon juice and garlic), baked aubergine or courgette slices, *tirosalata* (a cheese pâté), *skordalia* (garlic and potato purée), *kalamarakia* (squid rings dipped in batter and fried) and many more.

Fish: harbour restaurants are the best places to eat for those who love fresh fish, as this is a Greek speciality. Admittedly, the meal will be expensive due to the custom of choosing fish and paying according to weight, plus the fact that the Aegean has been overfished and so fish are not in plentiful supply, but visitors should treat themselves at least once.

Fish are usually grilled with a liberal sprinkling of fresh herbs and lemon juice. Red snapper and sea bream are well worth sampling. Greek chefs are masters in the preparation of lamb as well. It is usually braised in the oven with various seasonal vegetables.

Seasonal Fruit

Meal with a view

Main dishes: the many spicy dishes made from minced meat always provide good value. *Moussaka* (minced lamb with aubergines and potatoes) is probably the best known main Greek dish, but other similar dishes include *keftedes* (minced meat balls), stuffed tomatoes, stuffed aubergines and stuffed vine leaves. Grilled liver is delicious as is *stifado*, beef with onions roasted in a clay pot. Lemon segments are offered with nearly all dishes and when mixed with olive oil make a tasty sauce.

Desserts: this is often a seasonal fruit such as plump violet figs or red pomegranates, which the restaurateur picks from his own garden. For something a little sweeter, pay a visit to the bakers (*zacharoplastio*) as tavernas do not serve coffee and cakes. The pastries, whether tarts, cream flans or puff pastry filled with nuts, almonds, honey and cinnamon, fried in oil and swimming in syrup, are very sweet and high in calories.

Drink: meals are usually washed down with mineral water (*metalliko nero*) or beer (*bira*). Many western European brews will be on the menu including Henninger, Amstel, Heineken, Löwenbräu and Carlsberg as well as wine (*krasi*). Here the obvious choice is *retsina*, a white wine fermented in barrels coated with a pine tree resin, and served very cold. Many top-class unresinated wines are also available (*see page 77*). *Ouzo*, an aniseed-flavoured spirit similar to Pernod, is widely drunk, and served as an aperitif when mixed with a little water. *Metaxa* is the leading brand of Greek brandy with three levels of quality: three, five and seven stars.

Coffee: Greek coffee (*ellinikos kafes*), usually a Turkish mocha, can be prepared in a number of ways, but is always served in tiny cups, usually with sugar added. Greeks will ask for *sketo* (without sugar), *metrio* (medium sweet) or *gliko* (sweet). It is always drunk hot and never with milk. Coffee can also be prepared by boiling water and finely ground coffee powder together in a special aluminium or copper pot. The frothy, whipped and chilled Nescafé which is widely drunk is called *frappé* and makes a refreshing drink on hot days. Cafés in tourist centres will also serve cappuccino and espresso.

The kafenion

The *kafenion* or traditional Greek café is gradually dying out. In the cities, and Rhodes City is no exception, snack bars, pizzerias, fast-food restaurants, bars and discos have taken over. In country areas where people live at a more leisurely pace and follow a well-established pattern, this meeting-place, primarily for men, continues to occupy a central place in their lives. Customers discuss politics, religion and the rest of the world, read newspapers, play *tavli*, a type of backgammon, and drink coffee or *ouzo*.

The Captain's House at Lindos

Rhodian wine

Resinated Greek wine (*retsina*) has harmed the image of Greek wines, as the distinct flavour is not always appreciated. This is a bit unfair as the quality of Greek wines has improved recently and some could soon begin to compete with the Italian and French equivalents.

Many Greek wines are unknown outside the country, but that will change. Modern production methods are now being introduced and Greek vineyards have an advantage over central European ones. Pests have hardly affected Greek vines, so fewer chemicals are required. The Greek Wine Institute operates a strict monitoring system similar to the French *appellation contrôlée*.

Embona, with the Emery cellars, is the wine-producing capital of Rhodes and Embona wines are among the best on the island. The gentle, full-bodied Cava Emery red compares favourably with a Burgundy. Emery's top white wine is called Villaré. The proprietors use the Athiri grape, passed down from antiquity. Attempts have been made to grow the vine outside Rhodes, but none have succeeded. It seems to need the special micro-climate of the Ataviros mountain and the long sunny days. The biggest Rhodian wine-producing co-operative is known as CAIR, which produces 93 percent of Rhodes' wines, about a quarter of which goes abroad. Two of their quality wines are: the dry white Ilios and the rosé Chevalier de Rodes.

Local wine tasting

Eating out on Rhodes

Rhodes City

Alexis, Odhos Sokratous 18, Old town. Tel: 29347. The best fish restaurant in Rhodes City. **Argo**, Plateia Ippokratous 23–4, Old Town. Black mussels in wine and squid with cheese, onions and herbs. View of St Catherine's Gate. **Cleo's**, Odhos Agios Fanourios 17, Old Town. Tel: 28415. Good French and Italian cooking. Pleasant atmosphere and good wine list. **Dinoris**, Plateia Moussiou 14a, Old Town. Tel: 25824. Friendly family-run taverna. Fish dishes a speciality. **Kon-Tiki**, New town near Mandraki Harbour. Floating restaurant with international cui-

Eating out in Rhodes City

sine. **To Steki**, Asgourou, 5km (3 miles) south of Rhodes City. Tel: 62182. No menu. Huge trays brought to the table for diner to choose. Only open in the evening. **Taverna Kamares**, Odhos Agios Fanourios 15, Old Town. Tel: 21337. Hearty Greek fare such as moussaka, pastitsio and mixed grill platters.

Lindos
Symposion, Odhos Apostolou Pavlou. Tel: 0244 31260. Fish dishes of a consistently high standard.

Kolymbia
To Nissaki (Little Island) next to the beach. Tel: 0241 56360/56250. Serves the freshest langoustines and the tastiest squid. **Dimitris**, Tel: 0241 56233. Family-run concern at the end of the eucalyptus avenue. Serves genuine Greek fare such as baked aubergine and grilled lamb.

Lardos
The Lardos Garden Taverna, Main Square. Swordfish in white wine sauce and stuffed chicken with prawns.

Gennadi
Memories, by the beach. Tel: 0244 43202. For imaginative fish dishes such as *Mussels Saganaki* or *Dentex Ladelemono.*

Kamiros Skala
Pitropakis. Tel: 0246 41241. Said to be the best fish restaurant on Rhodes. Try grilled sea bream or red snapper.

Monolithos
Christos Corner. Adapted to the demands of tourists. Fine view over the sea from the terrace.

Embona
The Two Brothers' Taverna. Tel: 0246 41247. The Bakis brothers serve mainly meat dishes in large portions.

Symi
Better value than the tavernas by the harbour are those in Chorio. **Giorgos**, at the top end of the Kali Strata. Traditional Greek fare served on a terrace. **The Trawler** near the Plateia Tarsana in Yialos. Straightforward Greek dishes. The **Vapori Bar**, Yialos' first bar, serves cocktails and snacks such as home-made cheesecake. **Roula's Café** serves breakfast and quick snacks such as omelettes.

Khalki
Omonia on the promenade in Nimborio. A variety of starters and grilled dishes.

Shopping

Rhodes for the connoisseur

Many beautiful and tasteful items are available on Rhodes, despite the plentiful supply of cheap souvenirs. There is a wide choice of pottery such as vases, mugs and bowls and the famous Rhodian plates.

Arhangelos pottery

The most popular motifs are sailing ships, animals (jolly, colourful cockerels) and flowers, in particular the hibiscus blossom. Apart from the shops in the Old Town or in the potteries themselves along the road from Rhodes City to Lindos, Arhangelos is the island's main centre for pottery. There are shops in Rhodes City which produce some magnificent (and very reasonably priced) carvings from the wood of olive trees: caskets, tiny containers, perhaps in the shape of a fish, ornate collapsable tables and much more.

Leather goods are worth investigating, particularly sandals and belts which are produced on the island. Natural sponges in all shapes and sizes (*see page 63*) are sold by street traders. Most are brought over from Kalimnos, the only island where the dangerous trade of sponge diving continues, or from Sicily or North Africa.

Leather goods are worth investigating

If it is possible to think of winter under a blazing sun, there are more than a hundred fur shops on Rhodes. Coats and jackets, some still made from mink, but also sheepskin jackets with a natural lining, are imported from the northern Greek island of Kastoria, the centre of the Greek fur trade. Such items are reasonably priced and very fashionable but their quality can be disappointing. The dye on the leather can sometimes be uneven. Really good quality fur coats are a rare commodity, but by making a close inspection of what is on offer, it may be possible to find a bargain. The furriers will also make coats to measure and it is usually possible to negotiate a good price as competition is fierce.

There are countless jewellers in Rhodes City and it is easy to get carried away and spend a lot of money. Both Zolotas in Odhos Ethnarchou Makariou and Ilias Lalaounis in the Plateia Megalou Alexandrou in the old town are branches of top Athens jewellers. Lalaounis also have branches in Geneva, New York and Paris. Both supply jewellery of an unmistakable style, but prices are high.

For those looking for something less out of the ordinary, the many shops in the old town are certain to have something to suit: a beautiful, white, embroidered tablecloth with matching serviettes, some woven or crocheted fabrics or just a T-shirt. Counterfeit fashion goods have found their way to Rhodes and even long-established shops in the new town sell imitations of famous brands.

Embroidered tablecloths

The state-run shop (Casts and Reproductions) on the corner of Odhos Apellou and the Street of the Knights (Ippoton) near the museum is the place to go for something that recalls Rhodes' long history, an Aphrodite, perhaps. Clearly, the works of art are not originals but replicas of statues, busts, vases and similar items from the museums of Greece. If there is nothing on display that fits the bill, then it is possible to order from a catalogue. For lovers of art interested in modern painting, it is well worth taking a look in some of Rhodes' art galleries. Many of the artists who have work on display, such as Thasos Yannopoulos, are well-known in western Europe. His gallery is situated in Odhos Vorriou Ipirou. Another painter, Manos Anastasiadis from the island of Karpathos, has a gallery in the Street of the Knights (Ippoton), while the works of other modern painters can be viewed in the Art Gallery in Amochostou Street in the new town.

Food is also a good buy: black olives, excellent olive oil, pistachio nuts and Greek coffee make welcome gifts.

Traditional weaving

Nightlife

Rhodes City

The gardens beneath the Palace of the Grand Masters are the scene of *Son et Lumière* performances each evening from April to October. For full details ask at the kiosk or the tourist information offices.

Authentic Greek dancing by the **Nelly Dimoglou Ensemble** takes place every evening except Saturday in the Old Town Theatre (Theatro Palias Polis) at Odhos Andronikou. Dance troupes from the Greek mainland and other islands perform here too. The Rhodian Folk Dancing Theatre is a national institution, like the Dora Stratou Theatre in Athens where Nelly Dimoglou was once a pupil. The dancers tour the rest of the world in winter. In 1992, for example, Nelly and her dancers were invited to perform in Japan. From the middle of June to the middle of August she runs week-long dancing courses.

Popular venue for dancing

The **Grand Hotel Rhodes** in Akti Miaouli has a casino with Roulette, Chemin de Fer and Blackjack.

Cocktail bar in Rhodes

The new town of Rhodes offers a wide range of discotheques and nightspots which stay open until the early hours of the morning. There are more bars in one square mile than in London, Paris or Berlin...about 600 at the last count. *The* street for bars and discotheques is Odhos Alexandros Diakou. All have their own distinctive style but with one thing in common: they are all open-air. **Inkas** has a good disco atmosphere and **The Blue Star** has a reputation for good rock music. **Memphis**, opposite, does not just specialise in Soul, Reggae, HipHop and Rap, but its 'Memphis Milk Cocktail' is also well regarded. The **Underground** discotheque is popular with Britons and also offers a wide choice of beers. **Playboy Disco** in Leoforos Ialisou is currently very popular. At midnight, an extravagant light and laser show takes place. Elvis has been born again, or so it would seem, at **Presley's**, Odhos Dragoumi 27. Fifties and sixties music is this disco's speciality. **Zorbas** (Odhos Iroon Politechniou) and **Elli** (Akti Kountourioti) offer a distinctive Greek atmosphere with live *rembetika* and *bouzouki* music.

Lindos

The **Antika Bar**, Odhos Apostolou Pavlou. With a roof terrace has become something of an institution. It serves a good selection of cocktails. The Lindos locals prefer to shun the noisy bars and discotheques near the beach but the pick of the bunch are **Acropolis** with live dance music and the **Kiriakos Bouzouki Taverna** which has live Greek music every night.

A tempting invitation

Active Recreation

Even in antiquity, sport occupied an important place in Greek life. Many families produced generations of famous sportsmen. A phrase by the fable writer, Aesop, offers proof that sport was held in high regard on Rhodes. Why else did the show-off in one of his fables boast that he could outjump all the other competitors? When challenged with the phrase *Hic Rhodos – hic salta!* (Here is Rhodes – jump here!), he was obliged to withdraw being unable to match his words with deeds. This Latin tag is still used to refer to unproven claims.

Water sports

A windsurfer's paradise

The bays of Ixia and Ialysos are ideal for windsurfing, as is Prasonisi in the far south. The swell there would satisfy the most demanding surfer. Most of the large hotels offer windsurfing lessons. The Fun and Function Center in Ialysos has a good reputation and boards can be hired there. Rhodes is the biggest yachting centre in the Aegean and American sports journalists rank it as the fifth in the top 20 sailing regions. All types of sailing boats and yachts can be chartered with or without crews. For further information ask at the Yacht Agency Rhodes, Amerikis 26, tel: 22927 or 30504/05, fax: 233393. The NOR water sports club at the Elli beach in Rhodes City will also provide additional information.

Underwater diving with breathing equipment is only permissible near Kalithea under the supervision of the 'Dive Med Centre' (DMC). This 12-year-old company undertakes seabed surveys in the search for wrecks and treasure. The DMC organises diving courses up to the highest level. For further information, tel: 28040 or 33654. Boats used for deep-sea fishing are moored in Emborio harbour.

Golf

The 18-hole golf course at Afandou, open all the year round, is situated between the long beach at Afandou and the road to Lindos. Refreshments available in the club-house. Clubs may be hired; lessons are offered in English.

Cycling

Cycling is a perfect way to get about in Rhodes City and the southern part of the island where traffic is light. Before hiring a bike, however, it always a good idea to inspect it carefully to make sure it is really roadworthy. Several companies on the beach at Rhodes hire cycles.

Walking

Early spring and autumn are best suited to walking holidays. A stout pair of shoes and plenty of suntan lotion and drinking water are essential. It is not advisable to go alone and a good map is indispensable.

Beaches

The beaches on the east coast of Rhodes are more peaceful and better protected from the wind than those on the west coast, where the *meltimi*, a cooling breeze, blows. The beaches between Rhodes and Lindos and those in the towns themselves are very popular, but the miles of beach along the southern side of the east coast near Gennadi are less well equipped and much quieter.

Pallas Beach: This beach at Lindos with its rows of straw parasols only extends for a few hundred yards and can get very crowded in the summer months. The two beaches beneath the acropolis in the round Bay of St Paul are almost enclosed by rocks and are much quieter.

Koskinou and Faliraki: Two major hotel complexes stand alongside these two long beaches, but there is plenty of space and opportunities for water sports.

Tsambika: At the foot of the monastery hill on the east coast lies a long, sandy beach in a beautiful setting.

Plimmiri: At the southern end of the east coast and usually deserted, it can suffer from a surfeit of beach debris. Plimmiri has no hotels, just a small taverna.

Prasonisi: This sandy beach at the southern tip of the island has recently been discovered by windsurfers and until recently there were only two simple tavernas offering fresh fish meals. The beach is linked to a tiny offshore island by a sandbank.

Ialysos (Trianda): This long beach on the west coast is rather exposed to the *meltimi* and the strong winds are best appreciated by windsurfers.

Cape Fourni: This quiet shingle beach is situated close to the impressive Monolithos monastery on the west coast, set between cliffs and rocks.

Teeing off

Cycling can be a slog

Escaping the crowds

Getting There

By Plane

If travelling to Rhodes on a scheduled flight, it will be necessary to change planes in Athens and take an Olympic Airways internal flight from Athens West Terminal. The international airlines all arrive at Athens' East Terminal, but there are plenty of taxis and buses connecting the two. Charter companies usually fly directly to the island.

In the summer, there are regular daily flights to Athens from London and New York, thinning out during winter. From Athens to Rhodes takes about 55 minutes and there are four flights a day all year round.

Rhodes airport is situated 16km (10 miles) south of the town near Paradisi. The Olympic Airways Bus, which runs to complement Olympic Airways arrivals/departures is the most comfortable and economical way to get to Rhodes City. Tickets can be obtained at the Olymic counter inside the terminal building. The bus goes to the Olympic Airways City Office, which is centrally located at 9 Odhos Ierou Lochou. For the return journey, buses leave from here 90 minutes before departure time.

In addition, there is a regularly scheduled public bus for Rhodes City which stops outside the airport, as well as the more expensive option of taking a taxi.

By Boat

Daily car ferries ply between Piraeus (or Rafina) and Rhodes and tickets are available from the offices of the individual ferry operators. Return tickets are not issued and if a journey is to be interrupted, separate tickets for each section must be purchased (*see* also *pages 86* for information on the ferry companies). Piraeus harbour office, tel: 01 451 13 11.

Those arriving by ship don't have far to go, especially if they are bound for the Old Quarter, whose walls end at the port. A bus or taxi from the ship is hardly worth the fare.

By Car

For motorists driving their own car, the so-called Green Card (international insurance cover) is no longer obligatory, but it is still advisable to carry one. It is also advisable to take out comprehensive insurance.

Those wishing to hire a car can insure themselves before leaving home. Such a policy will cover against compensation due to third parties. The wearing of seat belts is compulsory on Rhodes. Maximum speed in built-up areas is 50km/h (31mph) and outside towns 80km/h (49mph). The permitted limit is 50mg of alcohol per 100ml of blood.

Make sure you're well insured

Getting Around

Island bus services are good

No shortage of taxis

A dog's life can be fun

Bring your own helmet

By Bus

Generally speaking, the island's bus services are good and it is not essential to hire a car. The terminus for the town buses is situated in Plateia Eleftherias. Almost all the villages can be reached by bus from Rhodes City. The stops are situated near the Nea Agora: Plateia Rimini for the east coast resorts and Averof Street for the west coast resorts. Fares are low and tickets are bought on the bus. Buses to the resorts run every 30 minutes, hourly to the interior of the island and to destinations in the south one to three times a day. To get to Lindos in high summer, take the Lindos Express. At weekends and on holidays, services are reduced. Raise an arm to stop a bus on the road.

Taxis

Rhodes is well supplied with taxis. Radio-controlled taxis are available around the clock (tel: 64712 or 64734). As fares are low, it is normal for drivers to stop for other passengers travelling more or less in the same direction. One taxi rank is in Plateia Rimini in Rhodes City, but taxis also wait at the airport and outside large hotels.

Car Hire

Rhodes is a big island and many visitors enjoy the freedom that a car provides. Hire cars are often badly maintained, so before signing the agreement it pays to check that everything works and that items such as the spare tyre are included. The road network is extensive, but roads in the interior are poorly surfaced creating a risk for tyres, which consequently may not be insured.

Visitors expecting to hire a moped or motor scooter should bring their own helmet, which are compulsory, however the hire companies often do not supply them.

By Ferry and hydrofoil

At least one ferry per day leaves Rhodes for Piraeus. There are three choices: a non-stop route, a route through the Dodecanese or a route via Crete. Ferries on the Dodecanese route stop at Kos, Kalimnos, Leros and Patmos; on the southern route at Karpathos, Crete, Santorini and Paros.

Other ferries link Rhodes with Rafina via the Cyclades islands. Several times a week boats sail to Kalimnos, Simi and Kastellorizo and once a week to Salonica. A car ferry service operates to Limassol in Cyprus and Haifa in Israel.

In the summer months, fast hydrofoils link Rhodes with Khalki, Tilos, Simi, Kastellorizo, Kos, Patmos, Samos, Leros, Kalimnos and Nisiros.

There are daily boat trips to Symi and Kos. Rhodes harbour office, tel: 0241 27690.

Postal facilities

Facts for the Visitor

Visas

Visas are not necessary to enter Greece, and British and American visitors can stay for up to three months.

Customs

From 1 January 1993 customs duties were lifted for travellers within the European Union and duty is not now payable on goods bought for personal use. If arriving from non-EU countries, the following quantities may be purchased duty-free on both the inward and outward journey: 200 cigarettes, 100 cigarillos, 50 cigars or 250g tobacco; 1 litre of spirits, strong liqueurs over 22 percent or 2 litres of fortified or sparkling wine, 2 litres of still table wine, 60g perfume or 250g toilet water

The export of antiques and icons more than 50 years old is forbidden.

The export of icons is forbidden

Tourist information

The Greek National Tourist Offices (EOT) overseas are:
In the UK: 195-197 Regent St, London W1R 8DL, tel: 0171 734 5997.
In the US: Olympic Tower, 645 Fifth Avenue, New York, NY 10022, tel: 212 421 5777.
611 West 6th St, Los Angeles, California 90017, tel: 213 626 6696.
168 North Michigan Ave, Chicago, Illinois 60601, tel: 312 782 1084.
Rhodes: at the corner of Papagou Street and Makariou Street, tel: 0241 23255 or 23655.
Rhodes City Information, tel: 0241 35945.
Lindos Information Office, tel: 0244 31428.

Currency and exchange

The Greek unit of currency is the drachma and notes to the value of 5,000, 1,000, 500, 100 and 50 drachma are in circulation. One hundred, 50, 20, 10, 5 and 2 drachma coins are used. Eurocheques should be made out in drachma to a maximum of 45,000 drachma. Many shops in Rhodes accept credit cards.

The drachma is not tied to the European Monetary System and the rates of exchange go up or down daily. In June 1994, all restrictions on exporting currency were lifted for EU passport holders. For residents of non-EU countries, there is no limit to the amount of foreign currency which may be imported, but exports are limited to 1,000 US dollars. Higher amounts may be taken out of the country as long as any imported monies were declared on entry. Individual travellers may import 100,000 drachma and export 200,000 drachma.

Lunchtime

Tipping

A service charge of 10 to 15 percent of the food bill is normally added in restaurants and tavernas. A small tip of 50 to 100 drachma is usual for waiters, taxi drivers, hotel staff and porters.

Opening times

Shops are usually open from 8.30am to 1.30pm and then again from 4.30 to 8pm, but many close on Monday, Wednesday and Saturday afternoon. In tourist areas, however, most shops are open all day and do not close until late in the evening.

Banks are open from Monday to Friday from 8am to 2pm. Museums and archaeological sites are open daily except Monday from 9am to 3pm. Lindos and Kamiros are open until 5pm. Monasteries usually close at 3pm.

Taking in the sights

Kiosks

Periptero are kiosks which sell many small items such as newspapers, cigarettes, toothpaste, sweets, combs, biros, stamps and much more. It is also possible to phone abroad from one of these kiosks. Some of them in the Mandraki district are open until late at night. The *periptero* by the Nea Agora sell foreign newspapers, but they are likely to be at least a day old.

Newspapers

A large selection of foreign newspapers are available from the kiosk by the entrance to the Nea Agora in Rhodes City, but they can also be purchased at most holiday resorts. They are usually a day late.

Local *What's On* guides in English can be found at kiosks and information offices.

Public Holidays

See Festival Calendar on page 73.

Postal Services

The postal service *(tachidromio)* and telecommunications (OTE) are not linked in Greece. Post offices are usually open from 7.30am to 2.30pm, but the General Post Office in Plateia Dimarchiou is open until 8pm and from 9am to 1.30pm on Sunday. Stamps are available in kiosks and souvenir shops, but a small surcharge may be made.

Post your letters here

Telephone

During the high season the main office for the Greek telecommunications company (OTE), situated on the corner of Odhos 25 Martiou/Amerikis, is open from 6am to midnight. It is possible to phone abroad from *peripteros* or from phone boxes with a white and orange livery. Some will take phone cards, which may be purchased from the OTE or kiosks. The code for dialling the UK is 00 44 and to the US and Canada is 001. AT&T, tel:00-800-1311; MCI, tel: 00-800-1211.

There are three different codes on Rhodes. For Rhodes City together with Afandou, Ialysos, Maritsa, Sguru, Soroni and Faliraki, the dialling code is 0241. Arhangelos, Gennadi, Kalathos, Katavia, Lardos, Lindos and Péfka numbers should be prefixed with 0244 and Apolakia, Eleousa, Embona, Monolithos and Salakos with 0246.

Phone box

Time

Greek time is two hours ahead of Greenwich Mean Time, seven hours ahead of Eastern Standard Time.

Voltage

Voltage is 220V.

Churches and Monasteries

Women are expected to cover their shoulders and knees when entering churches and should not wear trousers. Men should wear trousers in preference to shorts. If a church is closed, then ask at the nearest *kafenion* where the key is kept. It is usual to give the guide a tip. In the church – usually near the candle container – there will be a plate or box for a small offering.

Women should have their shoulders covered

Photography

Camera film can be very expensive in Greece and should be purchased in advance. In museums, photography (not flash) is permitted but a supplementary ticket may have to be purchased. At archaeological sites, photography is usually permitted, even with a tripod, but there is a fee, which can vary. Photography in churches is generally prohibited.

Topless bathing is no longer frowned upon

Nudism

Nude bathing is not generally tolerated on Rhodes and is advisable only on the remotest of beaches and on the naturist beaches near Faliraki on the east coast. Topless bathing, however, is no longer frowned upon.

Crime

Although holidaymakers should not take unnecessary risks with their property and valuables, like the rest of Greece there is little petty crime on Rhodes. Even women travelling alone need not fear unwelcome advances. Simply say *ochi* (no) very firmly to any persistent admirer.

Women are safe alone

Drugs

Visitors are warned that possession of or dealing in drugs, even small quantities of marijuana, is a punishable offence and can result in a prison sentence. Anyone found with large quantities of drugs could face several years in jail.

Medical

British and other EU nationals are officially entitled to free medical care in Greece, but this means admittance to only the lowest grade of state hospitals and the E111 form available from DSS offices must be produced. It is recommended that all visitors to Greece take out a travel insurance policy to cover illness. Most doctors have surgeries in the town centres.

Rhodes municipal hospital is situated in Odhos Erithrou Stavrou. There is an emergency service and a first aid post there, tel: 0241 22222.

Chemists: The Greek word for chemist is *farmakia* and these shops can be identified by the red Maltese Cross. While Lindos, Arhangelos and Lardos each have one pharmacy, in Rhodes City they can be found on virtually every street corner. As well as selling Greek medicines, most British medicines are available and are invariably cheaper than in the UK. Many of the medications which would require a doctor's prescription, such as penicillin and other antibiotics, are available over the counter.

Emergencies

Help is at hand

Police emergency in Rhodes City, tel: 104
Tourist Police, tel: 27423
Airport Police, tel: 92210
Harbour Police, tel: 27690/22220
Police emergency in Ialysos, tel: 92210

Diplomatic Representation

UK: Consulate, tel: 27247; Embassy, 1 Ploutarnou St, Athens, tel: 723 6211-9
USA, 91 Vas. Sofias Ave, Athens, tel: 721 2951-9

Accommodation

During the months of July and August it is essential to reserve accommodation, but at any other time of year, finding a room in a hotel or in a pension ought not to be a problem. Official statistics give the number of beds on the island as 60,000, but unofficially, the figure is nearer 100,000 and every year more become available. Prices during the low season are usually 30 percent lower than in the high season. The government regulates hotel prices and a notice giving tariffs should be on display in all rooms.

Towards the end of the season in October, the resorts south of Rhodes are more or less empty. Most hotels open from Easter to the end of October.

Luxury (L) and A category hotels in Rhodes are geared entirely towards the holiday trade. Certainly, the luxury hotels on the island rank among the best in Greece, fulfilling all the criteria that are demanded of hotels in this category. Standards and prices in the A category can vary according to situation, condition and facilities. Nearly all of them have swimming pools, tennis courts and other sports amenities, restaurants, bars and discotheques. Many provide play areas for children.

Big differences in price and other facilities exist among B and C category hotels. Although the EOT (Greek National Tourist Office) regulates the hotel classification system, it is not closely monitored.

Some hoteliers may prefer their establishment to be classified at a lower grade for tax reasons and it is often difficult to distinguish between many A and B category and B and C category hotels, apart from the price. To make it easier to gauge quality and to guarantee it, the government is planning to introduce a system for restaurants, hotels and other tourist amenities using symbols.

Welcome sign

Hotel with all amenities

Modern luxury in Trianda

Hotels in the D and E category are very basic and offer only rooms without breakfast. E category hotels usually do not have showers, but the family atmosphere can often compensate for the meagre facilities. Most C category hotels are family-run businesses. If holidaymakers are seeking accommodation but do not like the anonymity of modern hotel chains, they will find the C category hotels offer a more than adequate service.

The small hotels in Rhodes City Old Town offer reasonable accommodation with a pleasant atmosphere, but admittedly few have showers. Look out for the blue/white plaque at hotel entrances showing that the establishment has been monitored by the EOT.

Included in categories A, B and C are the rooms which are registered with the EOT, but many also let out other rooms at lower rates in order to avoid paying taxes.

Plenty of rooms to let

Here are some guide prices for overnight accommodation in a double room:

Luxury and A category: 16,000drs ($$$)
B and C category: 8,000drs ($$)
D and E: 4,000drs ($)

Camping: the only camp site on the island is near Faliraki (April to October, tel: 0241 85515 or 85358). It is extremely well equipped, offering shops, sports facilities and entertainment.

There are no youth hostels on Rhodes.

Sun Beach Hotel Rhodes

Rhodes City

Old Town: There are many small hotels and pensions here. Most are reasonably priced but offer only basic facilities with a wash basin in the room, communal toilets and no bath. Nevertheless, they are often quieter than the hotels in the new town and many offer fine views from their terraces.

$$Cava d'Oro. All 13 rooms have showers and toilet. The inner courtyard adjoins the town wall. In the old town. Odhos Kisthiniou 15, tel: 36980. **$Andreas.** 12 bright rooms with wash basins but no WC. But there is a fine view from the terrace over the old town and out to sea. Pleasant inner courtyard with palm trees. In the old town. Very quiet. Odhos Omirou 28d, tel: 34156.

New town/environs

$$$Grand Hotel Rhodes. Luxury hotel with 368 rooms and casino. Separated from the beach by the promenade. Akti Miaouli 1, tel: 26284, fax: 35589. **$$$Mediterranean.** 150-room hotel for those who give beach and night-life a high priority. Odhos Kos 35, tel: 24661. Near the aquarium in the new town. **$$$Rodos Bay.** Comfortable 330-room holiday hotel. Fine view over the Trianda Bay, Ixia. 5km (3 miles) from Rhodes City, tel: 0241 23661-3, fax: 21344. **$$Sun Flower Beach.** A smallish hotel with 70 rooms, tennis court and watersport facilities. Kremasti beach, 12km (7 miles) from Rhodes, tel: 0241 93514, fax: 94270. **$$Sabina.** Pleasant 70-room hotel with pool and tennis court. Friendly atmosphere with some non-smoking rooms (unusual in Greece). Theologos Beach, 7km (4 miles) from the Valley of the Butterflies, tel: 0241 41613, fax: 41681.

Lindos

In Lindos itself, the only available accommodation is in private houses and holiday flats. The tourist office situated in the main square will be glad to provide information on rooms. Alternatively, the Rhodes Express travel agency, Ethnarchou Makariou 45, Rhodes City, tel: 0241 31331, fax: 0241 73201.

Hotels are situated in the resort of Pefki (4km/2½ miles away) and also by Vlicha Bay (3–5km/2–3 miles) which has three largish, comfortable hotels. **$$$Lindos Bay** is the oldest and, with 400 beds, the biggest, tel: 0244 85107. **$$$Lindos Mare** was opened in 1992 and is a friendly hotel laid out on terraces, tel: 0244 31102 or 31130, fax: 31131. **$$$Steps of Lindos** certainly enjoys the best location. The 320-bed hotel is set into a hillside affording magnificent views across Vlicha Bay and Lindos, tel: 0244 42262-66, fax: 42267.

Lindos village: private accommodation

Koskinou

A number of large hotels are situated by the beach near Koskinou. **$$$Eden Rock** has been established for 25 years. It has over 400 rooms, good watersports facilities and bikes to hire, tel: 0241 23581-3. **$$$Paradise** is one of the best hotels in its category on Rhodes. The 630-room hotel lies in a sheltered bay and can offer bars, restaurants, a night-club, a discotheque, tennis courts and good watersports facilities, tel: 0241 66060, fax: 66066.

For those who prefer something a little less impersonal, the **$$$Virginia** with only 68 rooms is perhaps more acceptable, tel: 0241 62041. By Rhodian standards, the $$**Kalithea** with only 15 rooms, is very small but many visitors will feel at home there, tel: 0241 62498.

Kalithea

The delightful **$$$Castello di Rodi** is situated only 2km (1¼ miles) from the thermal baths. With only 60 rooms, it is both elegant and luxurious, offering a wide range of facilities, including swimming pool, sauna and lush gardens, tel: 0241 64856, fax: 64812.

Welcome to Faliraki

Faliraki

All the main hotels here are firmly in the hands of the major tour operators. Situated about 200m (220yds) from the beach, the 30-room $$**Mouses Hotel** is of a high standard, tel: 0241 85303.

Faliraki Camping (tel: 0241 85516, 85358) 16km (10 miles) from Rhodes City with a good bus service. About 1km (½ mile) from Ladiko and Afandou Beach. Superior facilities with swimming pool, restaurant, supermarket and discotheque.

Kolymbia

$$$Lydia Maris is a tastefully designed holiday complex with accommodation in 102 rooms centred on a huge swimming pool. Sports facilities include floodlit tennis courts. Popular with tour operators, tel: 0241 56294 or 56241-2, fax: 56424. $$$**Kolymbia Beach** is a smaller, well-maintained hotel with 65 rooms, tel: 0241 56225 or 56247, fax: 56203.

Arhangelos

Arhangelos

$$$Kariatides, a new hotel with 30 rooms, swimming pool and snack bar selling Greek specialities. 1km (½ mile) from the town centre, tel: 0244 22965. $**Antonis**, a family pension (7 apartments) next to the beach at Stegna. The landlord cooks occasionally, tel: 0244 22280.

Lardos

The 400-room $$$**Rodos Princess** was opened in 1993. Situated close to the beach at Kiotari, 5km (3 miles) north of Gennadi it has all the usual tourist facilities, tel: 0244 43102, fax: 43567. $**Fedra.** A simple, but clean hotel with a pleasant family atmosphere, in the centre of the village, tel: 0244 44218.

Gennadi

$$Dennis. Small, quiet apartment hotel in the C category, tel: 0244 43395. For those seeking extra facilities such as a swimming pool and a tennis court, try **$$$Lydian's Village**, a hotel complex (97 rooms) built like a Cycladian village, by the sea between Lardos and Gennadi, tel: 0244 44161-4, fax: 44165.

Studios at **$Panagos** in the middle of the town can also be rented. Small, with very pleasant gardens.

Kremasti

Apartments and studios of all categories are available to rent. The 74-room **$$$Iliotropio** is a very comfortable hotel, tel: 0241 93893 or 93514.

Kamiros Skala

$Artemis. Only seven tiny rooms without showers.

Monolithos

The **$Thomas** hotel has 30 rooms with refrigerator and kitchenette, tel: 0244 22741. Christos in the taverna lets out rooms and can supply other addresses.

Apolakia

$Skoutas, the only pension (9 rooms) is clean but very basic, tel: 0246 61251.

Salakos

$Nymphi with only four rooms, tel: 0246 22206.

Profitis Ilias

The 65-room **$$Elafos-Elafina** is open from May to September, tel: 0246 22225.

Symi

Many of the 15 rooms at the **$$$Aliki** are both stylish and spacious, tel: 0241 71665. The 9-room **$$$Dorian** offers similar accommodation. Both of these hotels are renovated Captains' houses near the harbour. **$$Grace** (tel: 0241 71415) with seven rooms and a good atmosphere, and the 11-room **$$Metapontis** (tel: 0241 71491) are both renovated villas. **$$Pedi Beach** in Pedi is a modern hotel with a pleasant atmosphere, tel: 0241 72176.

Symi Tours let holiday flats, tel: 0241 71307, fax: 71214.

Khalki

The **Captain's House** in Nimborio occupies a fine old house with an inner courtyard, tel: 0241 67201. **Nick's Taverne** by the beach at Pondamos, tel: 0241 57248. As both have very few rooms, a reservation is advisable.

Hotel in Gennadi

Pension in Salakos

Symi seen from the water

Index